I Am **NOT** Making This Up

AL STRACHAN

FOREWORDS BY
ROY MacGREGOR AND **WAYNE GRETZKY**

I Am NOT Making This Up

My Favourite Hockey Stories

FROM A CAREER COVERING THE GAME

Fenn Publishing Company Ltd.

TORONTO, CANADA

To Peter Loaring, without whom I wouldn't have been around to do this.

Fenn Publishing Company Ltd.

A Fenn Publishing Book / First Published in 2010

Copyright © 2010 by Al Strachan

Fenn Publishing Company Ltd.
Toronto, Ontario, Canada
www.hbfenn.com

The publisher gratefully acknowledges the support of the Canada Council for the Arts and the Ontario Arts Council for its publishing program. We acknowledge the support of the Government of Ontario through the Ontario Media Development Corporation's Ontario Book Initiative.

THE CANADA COUNCIL | LE CONSEIL DES ARTS
FOR THE ARTS | DU CANADA
SINCE 1957 | DEPUIS 1957

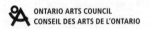

ONTARIO ARTS COUNCIL
CONSEIL DES ARTS DE L'ONTARIO

We acknowledge the financial support of the Government of Canada through the Canada Book Fund (CBF) for our publishing activities. Care has been taken to trace ownership of copyright material in this book and to secure permissions. The publishers will gladly receive any information that will enable them to rectify errors or omissions.

Library and Archives Canada Cataloguing in Publication

Strachan, Al
     I am not making this up : my favourite hockey stories from a career covering the game / Al Strachan.

ISBN 978-1-55168-388-1

     1. National Hockey League--Anecdotes.
2. Hockey--Anecdotes. 3. Hockey players--Anecdotes.
4. Strachan, Al. I. Title.

GV847.8.N3S85 2010   796.962'64   C2010-904513-0

Illustration: Anthony Jenkins
Text design and electronic formatting: Martin Gould

Printed and bound in Canada

10 11 12 13 14 5 4 3 2 1

Mixed Sources

Cert no. SW-COC-001271
© 1996 FSC

FSC

Table of Contents

Acknowledgements

A book like this can't be written without a lot of assistance. People like Gail MacDonald, Dave Carter, Pierre LeBrun and Lucie Leduc—as well as Alan and Leona Golding—offered insights and encouragement when they were needed most. Marian Strachan gave the raw manuscript her usual scrupulous examination and saved me from considerable embarrassment.

Roy MacGregor and Wayne Gretzky astonished me with their kindness—although I really shouldn't have been astonished. They've both been remarkably kind to me over the years. On the business side, Brian Wood got the project rolling and Jonathan Schmidt kept it on track. But it was the players of the National Hockey League who made the greatest contribution. Without their help and cooperation, none of these stories would have come to light. Working with and among them for more than three decades has been a pure delight.

And, as I have come to discover from writing books, there will probably be errors. If so, don't blame any of these people. The fault is mine.

Foreword by Roy MacGregor

You haven't lived—or died—until you've passed through a security line with Al Strachan.

"May I check your bag, sir?" the uniformed official will ask.

"Why don't I just show you where the bomb is?" he will sometimes answer.

Or: "What do you think I'm carrying in here—an Improvised Explosive Device from Afghanistan? A nuclear bomb? Box cutters? Or maybe just a musket?"

If it throws you off, it is nothing compared to the effect it has on the uniformed guard—usually a kid—under orders to check the bags going in for something that shouldn't be going in.

To a hockey game.

"Strach" is no fool—though he's been called worse—and keeps his unpredictable, wild and mischievous mouth shut when passing through airports. But just put him in one of those ridiculous "security checks" the National Hockey League instituted following the 9/11 terrorist attacks and watch out.

Some writers tilt at windmills; Strach tends to strafe them.

"Does it ever occur to you," he will ask the officials poking through his briefcase, "that we might be here to cover a hockey game, not blow it up?"

He has, in fact, been covering hockey virtually since muskets were the weapon of choice. He not only once carried a portable typewriter—a strange device that came without spell-check to correct your mistakes or Google to do your research—he has even filed by telegraph, an even stranger device that would take far too long to explain here.

He was there when Toe Blake was holding court on the Canadiens, there when a kid too skinny and slow showed up wearing No. 99 and made fools of the naysayers, there when the Broad Street Bullies were tamed, there when expansion spun out of control and there, most significantly of all, when the Gary Bettman Era began and Modern Hockey slowly morphed and twisted and bent and leapt and slid into what professional hockey is today, security checks included.

Al is the anti-Bettman, the voice of those who think the game should be played more on the ice than in the corporate offices. To say he has strong opinions is to say Buckley's is strong medicine. To say he is not worth hearing is to make a grave mistake, even when you might not always agree with him.

Take me, for example. His politics made Genghis Khan look soft; mine make Tommy Douglas look harsh. His perfect hockey game would have no referees, feature as many goons as shooters and have the medical staff busier than a big city emergency clinic; mine would have more whistles than players, feature only Europeans and permit only incidental body contact, as in women's hockey.

Okay, we're joking—but you get the sense. How, then,

could two such different people end up such good friends? And how could I end up with such huge admiration for Al Strachan as the consummate Canadian hockey writer?

Simple. It's about respect. I learned early on in the game of hockey writing that not very many of those who write about the game understand how it is actually played. Strach does. I also learned that there are no athletes as entertaining, warm and sincere as hockey players—no matter if they're from Northern Ontario or Northern Sweden—and Al Strachan has preached this reality since the first time he stepped into a dressing room. Not, please not, "locker room."

But it is far more than hockey. Al, despite his pretences to the otherwise, is as erudite and well-read as anyone I have known in the business. You want to talk naval battles, European history, economic theory—and please don't make the mistake of thinking I can carry my own in any of those fields—sit down with Strach. He'll have opinions just as strong in those areas.

He calls this book *I Am Not Making This Up*, and he's not. It is presented as snippets, but do not make the mistake of thinking this is bathroom reading or light fare. It is, in fact, several books in one:

It is a history—and a damned accurate one—of the Modern NHL from the 1970s to the second decade of the twenty-first century.

It is an analysis of the Bettman years that begins and leads a debate about the present and future of NHL hockey that all true hockey fans need to be engaged in—no matter where they might stand on recent developments.

It is a lament for the sportswriter's world that used to be, when you could sit and chat and actually get to know those you were covering and use that special knowledge to tell readers about personalities that might surprise and offer insights that might tell. It begins in a time when dressing rooms—not locker rooms—were places of reflection and discussion, long before they became so packed with cameras and microphones and bloggers and tweeters and now even the NHL's own dot-com writers that the players avoid their own stalls for fear of suffocation.

It is a collection of some of the funniest stories in hockey lore—bless you, Al, for finally getting the remarkable Dave Peterson–Klauss Zaugg confrontation down on paper.

It is an insider's account of what went wrong with *Hockey Night In Canada*, once the flagship hockey broadcast and today so often off-topic and out of touch with today's game. Bring back, please, the Hot Stove panel that used to feature insight and knowledge by the likes of Strachan and the *Globe and Mail*'s Eric Duhatschek. They are sorely missed.

I Am Not Making This Up is a lovely read, written by someone as likely to quote George Santayana as Dave "Charlie" Manson, and written well.

It is funny, affectionate, sharp—delivered in Strach's familiar, and appreciated, no-nonsense approach.

He pulls no punches; but he sure yanks a lot of chains.

Enjoy.

Foreword by Wayne Gretzky

When you spend years as a professional hockey player, you come to understand that the game itself is only one part of what makes the National Hockey League so good. For the game to have really good fans, it needs people who are able to communicate the everyday life of the game—its ups and downs, and its highs and lows. These are the things that the players go through all the time. Al has always been able to reach out to fans from coast to coast in two countries and make them aware of what that feeling at the arena really is— and sometimes let them in on the fun and heartache away from the arena as well. When you love the game as much as he does, no wonder he can write a hockey book that reads as smoothly as Jean Beliveau skated.

I really hope you enjoy reading the book!

Wayne Gretzky
99

Introduction

As far as I know, I was the world's first hockey columnist on a daily newspaper. Before that, there had been sports columnists. In fact, I was one myself. In that job—at least at the big papers—you opined on all the major sports, covered the big events and on slow days produced a "think piece."

But when I was working at the *Globe and Mail* in the mid-eighties, the managing editor, Geoffrey Stevens, asked if I'd be interested in focusing almost exclusively on hockey.

I never found out whether he made the suggestion because he liked my hockey coverage (he said he did, but managing editors lie a lot) or didn't like my coverage of other sports.

Either way, it sounded good to me. At the time, hockey players were by far the best pro athletes to deal with. In the other sports, the athletes thought they mattered.

Ask a baseball player what went wrong when he booted a double-play ball and you'll get either excuses or abuse. Ask a hockey player about a mistake and he'll not only admit his responsibility, he'll blame himself for a host of other flaws as well.

Athletes in the other sports tended to live in a hermetically sealed community that allowed entrance only to others of their ilk. That was not the case in the National Hockey League (NHL).

Assuming that the players knew you a bit, you were invariably welcome to join them for a beer or two, to travel on their bus, or just to stand around and chat about non-hockey matters.

All that has changed now, mostly thanks to National Hockey League commissioner Gary Bettman, who understands all the legal strictures of hockey but none of its camaraderie. Even players have to submit to metal-detecting wand scans on entering the arena now, and there's hardly anything more ridiculous than seeing the game's referee being told he must leave behind his toiletry bag because a security guard doesn't feel he can be trusted with a safety razor.

Travel has changed as well, so most visiting teams head for the airport right after the game. When I first became a hockey columnist, they headed for a local bar.

None of this alters the fact that hockey players—and the people of the entire hockey community with the possible exception of the NHL's head office—are highly entertaining.

The inside-hockey anecdotes are still available; it's just that they're not as easy to acquire as they once were. But what follows is a compilation of a number of those anecdotes, interspersed with some of the developments in the media business that affected the way the game was covered.

Some of the stories are funny. Some provide an insight into the mind of the professional hockey player. Some cover a historical aspect of the sport.

In every case, one thing must be made clear. I am not making this up.

ONE
Playing with fire

When Canada played Slovenia at the world championships in Innsbruck, Austria, in 2005, the game was a total mismatch. The Canadians took a relaxed approach to the proceedings and still won 8–0. For most of the game, they were on the attack.

But on one of the rare occasions when the puck went down to the Canadian end, a remote-controlled camera came loose from its mounting on a metal girder near the ceiling, fell to the ice and smashed to pieces in front of the Slovenian goaltender. To most people, it was a serious occurrence. The camera belonged to a Reuters photographer and shortly after it made its death dive, three Austrian police officers arrived in the press box to return the shattered remains and take a statement from its owner.

The International Ice Hockey Federation (IIHF), which runs the world championships, immediately banned the use of overhead cameras until further notice. In some sports, there would be no end of whining from the players, perhaps even threats of legal action. Canadian hockey players are a different breed.

Kris Draper, sitting on the bench, said to his teammates,

"It's a good time to be in your own end. You don't want to be on offence when cameras are falling."

After the game, Shane Doan was asked if he was worried.

"Oh, no," he said. "That's why the new CCM helmet is so thick. It has an extra pad in the forehead. In case a camera ever comes at you from that direction, you're safe."

• • •

Theoren Fleury's battles with alcohol over the years have been well documented, especially by Fleury himself in his excellent book *Playing With Fire*.

At one point during his career with the New York Rangers, he was on the NHL's watch list, having already been suspended for substance abuse, and there were reports in the media that he had been out late during a road trip to Montreal and had fallen off the wagon.

During the "Satellite Hot Stove" segment on *Hockey Night in Canada*, I confirmed that Fleury had been out later than perhaps a hockey player should, but I said that he hadn't been drinking.

I said that he had probably been at the ballet.

After the game, I was in a cab heading for a post-show meeting at a local watering hole when my phone rang. It was John Rososco, then the Rangers' media-relations man.

J.R. is a capable guy, among the best in the business, and he didn't bother offering his own opinion of the matter. He just passed along the message from the Rangers' GM at the time, Glen Sather.

"Glen is mad at you," he told me. "He's upset about what you said about Fleury. He wants you to call him."

Still in the cab, I called Sather. "What are you doing saying that Fleury was in a strip joint?" he asked. "The kid's trying to work through his problems and you're saying he's out watching strippers."

I asked Sather if he had seen the show. It turns out he hadn't, but he had been given a report.

Obviously, I pointed out to him, the report had come from a hockey person. I told him that I had simply said Fleury might have gone to the ballet.

To almost everyone in the world, the ballet is the ballet. In the NHL, the ballet is the Chez Parée strip club in Montreal.

Sather let the matter slide.

• • •

These days, Russian hockey players who think they're potential NHL material often study English before they get drafted by a North American team.

It makes good sense. The NHL game is demanding. If you don't follow a coach's orders, you won't be on the team for long. And it's hard to follow the coach's orders if you can't understand them. You could hope that one of your teammates is a Russian who can translate for you, but there isn't always time for that option.

The language barrier can cause some difficulties, but it can also provide a touch of humour.

During Jacques Lemaire's first stint as coach of the New Jersey Devils, one of his forwards was Valeri Zelepukin, one of the Russians whose knowledge of English was extremely limited. Zelepukin was well liked by his teammates and he tried his best, but not everyone is a linguist.

One day, when the Devils were going through a bad stretch, Lemaire gathered the players in the dressing room and started laying down the law. There were going to have to be improvements, he said. The team had to start playing the way he wanted them to play. Or else.

"We've not been playing well," he said, "and if we keep on playing like this, you know what's going to happen, don't you?"

He looked at the team. There was total silence. Heads were down. Then Zelepukin gingerly raised his hand.

"Coach get fired?"

• • •

As recently as the 1970s, there were NHL goalies who didn't wear masks. Today, every goalie not only wears a mask, he willingly uses it to stop shots.

"Absolutely," said Curtis Joseph, one of the NHL's greatest goalies of all time. "When you play goal, you lead with your shoulders a lot of times because you want to block everything. When they get into the areas that you can't react, you have to be a blocker, so you get out to cut down the angle. "If there's a deflection and you know it's going to be deflected, you'll put your head in the way."

The method isn't without its drawbacks, but goalies just shrug it off as an occupational hazard.

"Sometimes, your ears are ringing," said Joseph, "and there's the smell of burning rubber. You can actually smell the rubber burning when the puck hits and ricochets off— not all the time, just on that once-in-a-while occasion."

Still, there are some scary moments. "I was in Edmonton one night," said Joseph, "and I got a shot off the wire that bent the cage. That's fairly normal. Then I looked at the cage and I thought about it. Because of the distortion, the space between the bars had enlarged.

"There were just a couple of minutes left in the period and I asked the referee to grab that puck for a second and see if it fit through my mask.

"He comes over and tries it and says, 'Yeah, but just barely.' So I've got to play for the next two minutes knowing that the next shot can take my eye out."

As it happened, all turned out well. "We got through the next two minutes and then we changed the mask," chuckled Joseph. "But what are you going to do? You can't stop the game."

•   •   •

One night, when the Los Angeles Kings were playing in Edmonton, there was a loud *thunk* just as the period was ending. Referee Ron Hoggarth looked towards the spot the noise came from to see Edmonton defenceman Dave Manson standing over Kings forward Dave Taylor.

As the teams filed off the ice and Hoggarth skated backwards towards the corner of the rink where the officials exit, Taylor unloaded on him, but to no avail. At the same time, Kings coach Barry Melrose was screaming from the bench and waving his arms.

Suddenly, Hoggarth, using that sixth sense possessed by all referees, realized that the Zamboni, which uses the same entrance as the officials in Edmonton, was backing out onto the ice surface and was inches away from crunching him. He darted aside, offered a few choice words to the driver and left the ice.

When the next period started, Melrose called him over. "I was trying to warn you about the Zamboni," he said.

"I thought you were just complaining about the cross-check," said Hoggarth.

"Hell, no," said Melrose. "Anybody who can't see a damn Zamboni can't be expected to see a cross-check."

• • •

Toe Blake, the legendary coach of the Montreal Canadiens, always hated goalie masks.

Perhaps this was because of the battles he had waged with Jacques Plante over the use of masks, or perhaps it was just that he was a purist and didn't like to see the changes that were affecting the game in the seventies.

By that time, Blake's coaching career had ended, but he was still very much a part of the Canadiens organization. He would travel with the team during the playoffs and often show up at morning skates.

The coach of the era, Scott Bowman, idolized Blake and talked to him at least once every day during the hockey season.

He always talked to him after games as well. Even if the team was on the west coast, as soon as Bowman had finished his post-game interviews, he would head for a pay phone and call Blake to discuss the Canadiens' performance that night.

When the team was at home, Blake usually attended the games, and on those occasions, he would hold court in the press room before the game and between periods. The media loved to gather around him to listen to his stories and his opinions, one of which was that goalies should not wear masks. His primary argument was that a masked goaltender lost some of his ability to see the puck.

One night, Montreal goalie Michel "Bunny" Laroque was hit on the forehead by a screaming shot and had to leave the game even though he had been wearing a mask.

During the next intermission, someone pointed out to Blake that the mask had saved Laroque.

"If he hadn't been wearing a mask," Blake was told, "Laroque would have been seriously hurt."

"If he hadn't been wearing a mask," snapped Blake, "he would have seen the shot coming."

• • •

Like most hockey enforcers, Dave Manson was a treat to spend time with—once you were away from the rink.

He had a great sense of humour, a lovely wife and an appreciation of what hockey had given him. Best of all, he kept everything in perspective.

When he got traded from Montreal to Chicago in 1999, I wrote a column assessing the deal and said that Manson was in demand in the NHL because he had the ability to scare people. "Unfortunately," I wrote, "three of them are invariably behind his own bench."

There are hockey players who might get seriously angry at a crack like that, but Manson just laughed.

By the time he played his thousandth game, he was with the Toronto Maple Leafs. The Leafs honoured him before the game and we went out for a couple of drinks afterwards. "That's quite the accomplishment to play a thousand games, Charlie," I said. "Just think. If it hadn't been for suspensions, you could have had two thousand."

"That's enough of that, Strach," he said, before ordering

another round. He was with the Dallas Stars when they advanced to the Stanley Cup final against the New Jersey Devils in 2000. Coach Ken Hitchcock decided to keep the media waiting for a couple of hours for the mandatory game-day press conference because of some perceived slight his team had suffered, so we were hanging around the rink in midafternoon when I saw Manson in the concourse.

"What are you doing here?" I asked.

He said he had brought his son down to take him on the ice and teach him some tricks of the trade.

"He needs help to learn how to slash someone?" I asked. "Or is it the fine points of spearing and cross-checking?"

"He doesn't play like me," laughed Manson. "He's a good little player."

The curious thing about Manson was that years earlier, he had been cross-checked in the throat by Sergio Momesso and his vocal cords had been damaged. He spoke in a gruff, husky croak that is hard to describe. It was almost like a whisper, but he still managed to earn a few misconducts for things he said to officials that they heard over an arena full of fans, so to call it a whisper would be a bit misleading.

Manson always said that the damage to his vocal cords was not permanent and that when his career ended, he'd have the necessary operation and get his voice back.

But his career lasted sixteen years and by that time, the damage was irreparable. So he still croaks.

•   •   •

Today Jimmy Rutherford is the general manager of the Carolina Hurricanes, and every time I see him, I think of a line that he delivered many years ago that may be the single best one-liner I ever heard in a dressing room.

At the time, Jimmy was a goalie for the Detroit Red Wings—one of the last to play without a mask, as a matter of fact.

In that era, the Red Wings were easily the worst team in the league and were often referred to derisively as the Dead Things.

One night, late in the 1976–77 season, they arrived in Montreal, long since eliminated from the playoffs and a whopping 78 points behind the Canadiens, who were in mid-dynasty and the best team in hockey.

Before the game, I sought out Rutherford. "Gee, Jimmy," I asked him, "how do you get up for a game when you're 78 points behind?"

Rutherford looked stern. "Don't forget," he said, "we've got a game in hand."

• • •

A decade later, the Wings weren't an awful lot better. The 1986–87 Wings won more games than their 1976–77 predecessors, but they were notorious for their off-ice antics.

This was not a team that lacked interests outside hockey, and most of those interests involved activities that took place in bars.

There were seven or eight guys on that team who rarely went to sleep sober, and coach Jacques Demers didn't know what to do. He wanted to crack down, but these guys were good players and the Wings were not without the occasional on-ice success. If a coach suspends his players and the team starts to lose, we all know what will happen to the coach.

Finally, though, Demers knew he had to put his foot down, so when Petr Klima and Bob Probert showed up late for a practice one day, he decided that he had had enough. He had to make an example of someone and these two had just qualified for that dubious distinction.

He called them into his office and told them bluntly—and at length—what he thought of their attitude. To teach them a lesson, he said, he was going to send them to the Wings' farm team in Adirondack, New York. Once they had made it clear that they were truly remorseful for what they had done, they could return to Detroit. Not before. Off they went.

A few days later, Demers called in assistant general manager Nick Polano. "Do you think those guys have learned their lesson yet?" he asked. "Do you think they're ready to come back and take the game seriously?"

Polano had no idea, so Demers suggested that he phone Bill Dineen, the Adirondack coach at the time, and find out how the two were playing.

Later, Demers approached Polano. "Well," he demanded, "have those guys changed their attitude? Are they playing well enough to come back?"

Polano didn't know how to soft-pedal the news, so he simply told the truth. "They're not there yet," he said.

It seems that Probert and Klima had stopped off in New York City to sample some of the nightlife and never did get to Adirondack. Polano was dispatched to New York to round them up and get them back to Detroit without further mishap. The Adirondack experiment was given up as a bad idea.

•   •   •

Petr Klima never was known for his ability to respond to discipline. Even though he was extremely talented, the Wings eventually decided that they could put up with him no longer and shipped him off to the Edmonton Oilers, a team that had a well-deserved reputation as being easy to play for.

The Oilers kept the rules to a minimum and asked only that the players work hard on the ice. But Klima couldn't do that, and the coaching staff got sick of his lackadaisical attitude. They made Klima a healthy scratch and forced him to sit out for more than a week, riding the bike every day.

Finally, the media descended on Klima and asked if he thought he was about ready to return to the lineup and play some serious hockey.

"I don't know about playing hockey," shrugged Klima, "but I'm ready to enter the Tour de France."

• • •

To me, Sam Pollock was the best general manager in NHL history. There have been others who have come close, but it was Pollock who was the true innovator. He was the one who developed the principles that the later guys followed.

Because I covered the Montreal Canadiens in the 1970s when the team's dynasty was at its zenith, I was occasionally exposed to the Pollock wisdom.

It would be wrong to suggest that we were inseparable. For the most part, you didn't see Sam. He had an office on the second floor of the Montreal Forum and spent most of his days there. He left the coaching to the coach—not a bad idea since, for the most part, the gentleman in question was Scott Bowman. Sam and his wife, Mimi, watched the games from red seats near centre ice, not the press box.

But should the team encounter a bad stretch—which for the Canadiens in those days was a close loss and a couple of ties—Sam would show up in the dressing room after the game.

The Montreal press (they weren't really "media" in that era because TV and radio didn't have the same kind of intensive coverage that they have today, but there were enough that we can call them that) were not known for their patience, and rather than leave Bowman alone to handle the baying hounds, Pollock would come down and make himself available.

But once in a while, maybe during the playoffs or at a team function, you would get a chance to talk to Pollock alone. He didn't like to say much for attribution—the running joke among the media was that if you asked Sam what time it was, he'd tell you only if you promised not to quote him—but he would answer the occasional question.

It was his policy to deal superfluous players to expansion teams for draft picks. That's how he got Bob Gainey, Guy Lafleur, Doug Risebrough, Mario Tremblay and a host of others.

To many of us, it seemed that the expansion teams never learned. They were forever trading away their future and enriching the Montreal dynasty. On one of those infrequent opportunities when I had a chance to ask Sam about his tactics, I wondered aloud why the GMs of these teams were so stupid.

Once we had agreed that his answer was not to be quoted, Sam said that the trading of draft picks wasn't necessarily stupid. If, after the season, you traded your fourth overall pick for a veteran, for example, that was fine. You knew what you were giving away and you knew what you were getting. After that, it was simply a matter of evaluating the two commodities and deciding if the deal made sense.

What was stupid, Pollock said, was trading away your draft pick when you didn't know what you were giving away. The draft order is based on inverse order of regular-season finish, so if you finished first, your first-round draft pick wasn't worth a lot. But it sure was if you finished last.

After Sam had acquired the Oakland Seals' first draft pick in 1971 (for Ray Martiniuk), he gleefully watched as the Seals wallowed in the basement. But when the Los Angeles Kings went into a tailspin and were in danger of sinking lower than the Seals, Sam quickly made the Kings a virtual gift of Ralph Backstrom, a quality player who kept them out of last place.

The Seals therefore finished last; Pollock got their first-round pick, the first overall, and used it to select Guy Lafleur.

• • •

Over the years, the good general managers learned from Pollock and became much more careful about trading first-rounders. They either waited until the season was over so they knew their standing in the draft process and therefore what they were trading away, or they threw in qualifying clauses, such as the right to delay the pick for a year if their team finished worse than expected.

Apparently, this was not a lesson learned by Brian Burke, who, in the summer of 2009, traded the Toronto Maple Leafs' first-round picks in 2010 and 2011—as well as a second-rounder—to the Boston Bruins for Phil Kessel.

No doubt Burke was, convinced the Leafs would not

finish low enough to lose a high draft pick. After all, they had a genius for a general manager. But that's not the way it worked out.

In fact, the Leafs finished 29th in a 30-team league. A trade that was highly suspect to begin with therefore evolved into a full-scale disaster. The top two players in the draft, Tyler Seguin and Taylor Hall, were both projected to be franchise players.

The Leafs would get neither. Instead, they had Kessel, a quality player but not one anybody (with the possible exception of Burke) considered to be a franchise player.

It brings to mind George Santayana's famous dictum "Those who cannot remember the past are condemned to repeat it."

Or perhaps "Those who think they are smarter than Sam Pollock deserve what they get."

• • •

For decades, Don Wittman, who died in 2008, was the CBC's all-purpose announcer. He could do everything from curling to hockey to Olympics. And he did.

He loved to gamble, and during the playoffs in the 1980s, when, as you might imagine, we spent a lot of time in Edmonton, we'd often visit the casino in the afternoon.

It was only a few blocks from the hotel, and Don liked to go for a couple of hours between lunch and game time. I didn't mind tagging along. The option was to stay in the hotel and play gin rummy with him. Invariably, the casino cost me a lot less. Witt was also a golfer, and he told me that one summer, he went to Scotland and managed to get himself a starting time at the famous old course at St. Andrews.

Unless you're physically handicapped, you can't use a cart at St. Andrews. You have to use a caddy, usually one of the wizened old veterans who has seen everything on the course. (Well, almost everything. After one of my more creative shots, my caddy confided in his deep Scottish brogue, "I've no been in this part of the course before.")

As Wittman strode up to the first tee, his caddy cast a discerning eye over him and asked, "And what's you handicap sirrrrr?"

"Eight," announced Wittman.

"Eight is it?" responded the caddy. "Let me see you take a couple of practice swings."

Wittman did as he was told.

The caddy watched him closely. "You must be a hell of a putter," he said.

• • •

Until Wayne Gretzky arrived on the west coast in 1988, the Triple Crown line—Charlie Simmer, Marcel Dionne and Dave Taylor—had been the only reason eastern hockey fans had paid the slightest attention to the Los Angeles Kings.

Perhaps that's not entirely true. Every so often, someone would ridicule their outrageous uniforms: hideous purple on the road and cheap-hooker gold at home.

When Simmer got married to Terri Welles, a centrefold in the December 1980 issue of *Playboy* magazine and Playmate of the Year in 1981, he became the envy of many NHL players—and also the target of a few off-colour remarks.

Simmer took it all in his stride. He was, and still is, an easygoing guy with a good sense of humour.

But in those days before satellite television, not many

people in the east knew much about him, so he seemed to
be a good subject for a feature in the *Globe and Mail*. As a
result, one Sunday morning when the Kings were visiting
Winnipeg, Simmer and I had breakfast.

At one point in the interview, I asked him about his
hometown and he identified it as "Terrace Bay, Ontario,
where men are men and so are half the women."

This was an era in which hockey writers used to help
themselves to other writers' quotes, so as the season went on,
the Terrace Bay–women quote appeared in more and more
papers.

Then one day, Rod Beaton of *USA Today* ran a note saying
that the widely used line attributed to Simmer had been a
misquote and that Simmer had not said any such thing.

Beaton was a good friend, so I asked him where he got
that idea. He said that Simmer himself had told him.

A few weeks later, I ran into Simmer somewhere and
said, "Charlie, how can you say that line about Terrace Bay
isn't true? You gave it to me that morning we had breakfast
in Winnipeg."

"Yeah, I know, Al," he said. "Sorry about that. But once it
started to get around, my mother started to get abuse from the
other women in Terrace Bay, so I had to deny I ever said it."

•   •   •

Earning a large NHL salary is generally a pleasant experience,
but it can also have its drawbacks.

During the summers, Teemu Selänne used to get
involved in car rallies in his native Finland. The sport often
requires high-speed driving on back roads, so Selänne and
two teammates decided to do some practising on a road that

they thought would be closed off.

There was apparently some confusion on this point and their car was involved in a collision. "We went on this private road and we didn't know we had to call the cops and say we were practising there," explained Selänne.

It was a matter of misunderstanding, not malice, but, nevertheless, Selänne and his friends were all charged with the same offence, to which they pleaded guilty. In Finland, the fines vary according to the income of the guilty party. Selänne's two friends were students whose incomes were negligible. Therefore, one was fined $55 and the other $75.

Selänne got fined $55,000.

• • •

In the 1988 Olympics in Calgary, the coach of the United States hockey team was Dave Peterson, a man who disliked the media, non-Americans and facial hair. Therefore, Klauss Zaugg had three strikes against him from the outset. Klauss didn't care. He worked for *Blick*, a paper in Switzerland, and tabloids in that part of the world are not the least bit concerned about the sensitivities of their intended subjects.

Peterson had a reputation as being difficult—especially towards the media—so we all looked forward to the press conferences featuring Peterson and Zaugg.

In the National Hockey League, the coach usually holds his post-game press conference in the hall outside the dressing room. But the press conferences for Olympic hockey were always held in a large auditorium with the coach and/ or the stars of the game up on the stage. An International Olympic Commitee (IOC) flunky roamed the crowd with a microphone that the media could use to ask questions.

In every game, the Americans either won in an unimpressive fashion or lost. On each occasion, in the post-game press conference, Klauss would grab the media microphone and boom out, "Coach Peterson! Will you now resign in shame?" Peterson would assert that he would do no such thing; Klauss would offer his condolences to fans of American hockey and that was that. Finally, after the Americans absorbed the defeat that eliminated them from further competition, Klauss started with his usual question.

"Coach Peterson! Will you now resign in shame?"

Peterson, clearly angry, said he would not and asked if there were any more questions. Klauss wasn't finished.

"Coach Peterson! Juan Antonio Samaranch [the head of the IOC at the time] said this morning that it is a shame that the American hockey team produced such a poor performance when the tournament is being held in North America. What do you have to say about that, Coach Peterson?"

"Juan Antonio Samaranch said that?"

"Yes, he did, Coach Peterson."

"Does Juan Antonio Samaranch know anything about hockey?"

"Do you, Coach Peterson?"

To gales of laughter, Peterson stormed off the stage and ended the press conference.

TWO

You've come a long way, Colie

One of the most delightful guys in hockey is Colin Campbell, the NHL's senior vice-president and director of hockey operations.

He has come a long way since his days on Team Cement Head, a dubious honour that will be explained later. Today, Colie, as everyone calls him, has to look serious and concerned as he tries to extricate the NHL from yet another looming PR disaster. Whether it's an officiating controversy, an ugly incident on the ice or the imposition of an unpopular rule, Colie is the guy who has to pacify the anti-hockey faction of the media.

When you watch him on TV, you see another suit, another totally corporate, humourless NHL executive.

It's all a facade. He is a committed hockey man; there's no doubt about that. He loves the game; he has been in it all his life and his son Gregory played for the Florida Panthers until signing with the Boston Bruins in the summer of 2010.

But humourless? Corporate? If you think that's the case, talk to some of his teammates on the Vancouver Canucks back in the early 1980s. The trainer of the team in those days was Larry Ashley, who had been with the organization so long that he was there even before it entered the NHL.

As often happens, Campbell and Ashley got into one of those feuds where each tries to outdo the other with a practical joke.

Ashley felt that he was on firm ground in this kind of battle. He was a fixture with the organization. He would never be fired. Imagine his surprise, therefore, when during the off-season, he got a letter from general manager Jake Milford informing him that he was being let go.

He stormed down to the Canucks offices only to learn that Milford was on vacation. No one could be sure Milford had sent the letter, but it had come in a Canucks envelope and had been written on Canucks stationery.

Because Milford was in Europe, Ashley spent a long time stewing and waiting for him to be tracked down before it finally became evident that the whole thing was nothing more than a practical joke engineered by someone who had access to team offices and had helped himself to some stationery.

The culprit, of course, was Campbell.

• • •

Ashley was far from Campbell's only target.

There was also the time when the team was on the road and one of the Canucks was stopped by airport security and told to dump out the contents of his carry-on bag. Out came an avalanche of hotel cutlery, soaps, shampoos, toilet paper, ashtrays and other purloined items that were as much a surprise to the hapless player transporting them as they were to the security staff.

Everyone on the team knew who deserved the credit/blame for that one.

On another occasion when the team was on one of its

endless meandering road trips through the east, the bus that was supposed to take the players from the airport to the hotel didn't show up.

In those days, the coaches had to do double duty as travelling secretaries, so Roger Neilson headed for the nearest bank of pay phones to track down the missing bus.

At the time, the airport was undergoing some renovations, and a lot of building material was lying about unguarded. When Neilson returned and picked up his bag, he almost dislocated his shoulder. Someone had put a cement block inside it. Neilson knew exactly who to blame and often did so in telling that story over the years. By then, he was laughing. But he wasn't at the time.

• • •

In the 1982 playoffs, the Canucks beat the Calgary Flames in the opening round, then took on the Los Angeles Kings. They won the second game when Campbell, to the astonishment of all concerned, scored in overtime.

He retrieved the puck and put it on display in his stall— at the front of the ledge for extra prominence. Any reporter expressing the slightest interest was handed the puck.

Once again, you have to remember that in that era, sports-highlights shows were not a part of television schedules. Very few people would have seen a replay of the goal.

To fill what he saw as a gap in the media's appreciation of his skills, Campbell had applied white adhesive tape to the puck and written all the relevant details on it. The time and date of the goal were there, as well as the final score. In addition, there was a lengthy description of the goal itself—how Campbell had stickhandled around a couple of defenders, taken the puck behind the net, avoided a check or two, stick-handled his way back in front, faked the goalie down and fired a beautiful rising shot into the upper corner.

In reality, he had floated a desperation shot from the point that had bounced on the way in, deflected off a skate and dribbled into the net.

• • •

Being a hockey columnist isn't necessarily a job that makes you feel proud. You can live with that. But that doesn't mean you want to be ashamed of your profession. At times, however, you have no choice. One such occasion occurred in 2006 when the Wayne Gretzky "gambling scandal" broke.

I was in Las Vegas covering the NHL general managers' meeting at the time. It seemed a bit ironic that the GMs, who had selected a gambling haven for their annual meeting, were being asked their reaction to an illegal-gambling story. But the day had hardly begun when I got a call from my employers at the *Toronto Sun* and was told to get to Phoenix as soon as possible.

"Gretzky and his wife and Rick Tocchet have been caught gambling on games," came the breathless announcement.

"I doubt that," I said.

"Well, the New Jersey police are going to lay criminal charges against them all, and organized crime is involved. Get over there and see what Gretzky says."

To me, this seemed stupid on a number of levels. For one thing, Gretzky would never get involved in anything like this. For another, most forms of gambling are not illegal, especially in New Jersey. It is the home of Atlantic City, after all. For another, if you want to gamble, it's easy to do it

online. You don't need to deal with a real-life version of Tony
Soprano.

Unfortunately, however, most of the media approached
the story the same way the *Sun's* sports editor did. Gretzky
had to be guilty. His wife was guilty. The Coyotes assistant
coach, Rick Tocchet, was guilty. They were a blight on sports.
They were despicable. They should be banned for life.

It was a full-scale, maximum-voltage media feeding
frenzy with inaccurate stories feeding off inaccurate stories
and pushing them even further from reality. I flew to Phoenix
and drove over to the arena. The Coyotes were to play that
night, but I was assured that Gretzky would talk to no one
from the media until after the game. No exceptions.

By this point, since game time wasn't that far away, I just
sat in the hallway near the Phoenix dressing room and read a
book. Not much later, Gretzky showed up flanked by a pair
of burly security people. They started to close in on me as I
approached, but Gretzky stuck out his hand.

"Hey, Strach," he said. "What's up?"

"They sent me over from the GMs' meeting to do
something on these gambling charges."

"Sure," he said. "What do you need to know?"

I asked the relevant questions, got all the answers I
needed and filed a story that went right onto the *Sun's*
website roughly five hours before the post-game press
conference. I went to that too, just in case there had been
any further developments. There weren't, but as he usually
did in situations of this nature, Gretzky came over to see if I
needed anything else.

I told him I didn't.

"What are you going to do now?" he asked.

"Nothing much. I've got to talk to a couple of guys, but it won't take long."

"Well, after you're finished, come on over to the house for a couple of beers."

At this time, four of Gretzky's children were with Janet in Los Angeles. The only one living with him was his son Ty who was fifteen. There was also a guy whose name I forget, a tennis coach from Australia. He was staying at the house for a while, but that was to be expected. There's always somebody who's not part of the family hanging around Gretzky's kitchen. One time it was Denis Leary, but that's another story.

So we all stood around the kitchen counter and chatted about what was going on. On the subject of gambling, Gretzky said, "I go into the Vegas casinos once in a while, but I don't even go into the sports book, let alone place a bet there. I would never bet on sports, but Janet is from St. Louis. She was betting on the NFL long before she met me. I keep telling her not to, but what are you going to do? Anybody who's married knows the answer to that."

Ty, who had been listening intently, spoke up. "That's right, Dad," he said. "When she gets on the phone with Rick, you go like this"—he threw up his arms and let out a sigh of exasperation—"and walk out of the room."

It was such a good impersonation that we had to laugh. But it was also so honest and so forthright that if I had ever harboured any doubts about Gretzky's involvement—which I hadn't—they would have been dispelled right there.

This is a man who has always taken great care to protect not only his own image but also that of the game he loves.

He would never place himself in a situation that could possibly leave a blot on his reputation. For instance, if he's in an elevator alone and a woman comes in, he gets out. If the two were to be in a closed elevator together, who knows what she—or anyone else—might say later?

On one occasion, when I was going to visit him at his Los Angeles home, which is in a gated community, I was a bit early and he hadn't had the opportunity to tell the guard I was coming.

"I'm sorry, sir," he said, "I can't let you in until Mr. Gretzky calls. I might do it for some people, but Mr. Gretzky is the nicest person in this entire community and I wouldn't want to do anything to upset him."

Yet this is the man the media publicly eviscerated without knowing any of the facts.

It's at times like that when you feel ashamed.

• • •

Gretzky has told me a lot of things over the years, many that weren't public knowledge.

But this one didn't come from him. It came from a close friend.

The story is that the night before the gambling revelations broke, Gretzky knew what was about to happen and called NHL commissioner Gary Bettman to bring him up to speed.

He also assured Bettman that although Tocchet and Janet had been involved to varying degrees, he himself was completely clean. He knew that Bettman would be besieged by the media the next day, and he wanted Bettman to say that while it was his duty to investigate thoroughly, he was sure that Gretzky was not involved.

Bettman did no such thing. He said everyone would be

exposed to a full-scale investigation, including Gretzky. No vote of confidence was forthcoming.

Gretzky was furious. His name was sullied with the others, and to this day, one still occasionally hears uninformed smartass remarks linking Gretzky to gambling.

The relationship between Gretzky and Bettman has been cold ever since.

• • •

On Sundays, Brodie Snyder rarely spoke.

When I started at the *Montreal Gazette* in May 1973, Brodie's official title was assistant sports editor, but, in fact, he ran the sports department. For that matter, he ran much of the rest of the paper as well. He was a hard-bitten old-school newspaperman, the best desk man I ever came across, and to the credit of others in management level at the *Gazette*, he was often called upon for advice by other departments.

I was hired as a desker too, one of the drones who edits stories, writes headlines and lays out pages. Because the *Gazette* didn't publish a Sunday edition in those days, Saturday was our day off. Then we would all troop in on Sunday afternoon, try to shake off our hangovers and put together the Monday-morning paper, which usually contained the biggest sports section of the week.

By late 1973, after six months or so at the *Gazette*, I had become quite familiar with Brodie's eccentricities. If he had to talk to someone on the phone, he would do so with a minimum number of words. When his wife made her nightly call around six o'clock, she got the same treatment—mostly grunts and one "No, not late," even though everyone at the paper knew it would be close to dawn before Brodie rolled out of the press club and headed for home on the West Island.

On Sundays, Brodie rarely issued more than a grunt to anyone in the office. Monday might produce a syllable or two, and as the week progressed, he would become increasingly sociable.

Three or four of us sat around a tangle of desks, each with an old Remington typewriter at his side. Brodie would slide stories over to us—either written by staffers or sent by teletype from a news agency like Canadian Press or United Press International—and we would edit them and slide them back. Each story would have Brodie's pencilled instructions regarding the kind of headline we were to write for it.

Every so often, Brodie would attack his Remington with a vengeance, rip out the half-sheet of copy paper that had been subjected to his assault and fire it across the desk in someone's general direction.

Usually, it was just some sort of instruction. "Call Ian and see when he's going to file," or "Go and find out how much room is left for us on the obit page." That sort of thing.

But one Sunday night, after a heated exchange with the hockey writer—which had ended in the usual fashion with the phone being slammed down—the half-sheet of copy paper he fired across at me contained a query: "Can you go to Los Angeles with the Canadiens tomorrow morning?"

I put a fresh half-sheet of copy paper into my Remington (since Brodie wasn't big on conservation), typed out a one-word affirmative answer and slid it back.

Thus began my career as a hockey writer.

• • •

I had come to the *Gazette* after spending three years at the

Windsor Star, covering general news, business, courts and so on. I also had done a stint as a copy editor on the desk. Following a summer course in French at Laval University in Quebec City, spent, largely, learning how to order food and drink and swear impressively, I applied for work in Montreal.

The managing editor of the *Gazette* said he was willing to hire me and, during the interview, asked if I spoke French. When I said that I could get by, but was certainly nowhere near being fluent, he decreed that I'd have to go into the sports department.

Knowledge of French wasn't really a prerequisite there, and I was only going to be working on the desk anyway.

To a kid out of Windsor, Ontario, the *Gazette* was the big time and I had a feeling of trepidation. The guys at the *Windsor Star* had not been noted for their professionalism, and the best way to gain the respect of your peers there was not to break a major story, but to stage some sort of elaborate and successful practical joke.

One guy, who had done nothing for weeks but talk eagerly about his upcoming trip to England, was asked to write a headline for the wire-service bulletin announcing an airline strike that would cancel all flights for at least a month.

The story had all the usual incomprehensible wire-service coding at the top and looked genuine in every way. It wasn't. We all got a good chuckle out of his reaction. On another occasion, the same guy, who was rather large, came back from a washroom break to find that his chair had been wired to another to double its size. But I was confident that this sort of impropriety would not be tolerated at the highly respected *Gazette*.

I started work on a Monday in early May, and on Wednesday afternoon, the baseball writer staggered in. The Expos were in town, but they had an off-day, so he had come into the office to write his story. There were no computers or e-mail in those days, just typewriters and paper. You couldn't work from home on the off-days as most sportswriters do today.

He pulled a chair up to one of the Remingtons, took a deep breath and collapsed face-first onto the keyboard. Brodie, who bore a remarkable resemblance to Jabba the Hutt in *Star Wars*, looked up from his desk and watched for a minute.

"Wow," I thought. "This guy is really for it now. This sort of thing might happen in Windsor, but not at the *Montreal Gazette*."

Sure enough, Brodie quickly sprang into action. It being Wednesday, he would occasionally toss out a few words. He looked at me, looked at the baseball writer and said, "Better close the door."

I did. Now the sports department was closed to prying eyes. Not sure what would happen next, I continued with my work, trying not to be distracted by the snores.

I knew that Brodie wouldn't let this situation go on forever. Sure enough, he didn't. After a while, he fired the latest set of Montreal Expos statistics across the desk, along with a note on the mandatory half-sheet of copy paper.

"Write an Expos story."

Baseball stories were about three pages long, so I banged out some drivel about the length of the latest Expos losing streak, how they hoped to turn their fortunes around, how different players had performed in the last few days and so on.

I kept thinking that the baseball writer might wake up soon and do his job, thereby sparing our readers from this inanity, but he continued to snore at his typewriter.

Finally, I finished the story and slid it back across the desk for Brodie to edit. He took his pencil, wrote the baseball writer's byline across the top and went to work editing it.

Then he stuck it in the out-box for the copy boy to take to the composing room.

So the first sports story I ever wrote appeared under someone else's name.

•   •   •

It must be mentioned that the baseball writer in question was excellent at his job, but like so many of us in the profession in those days, he enjoyed relaxing with a "few."

On that day, Brodie stood up around 6:30 p.m., as he usually did, and announced that he would be next door at Mother Martin's, the favourite pre-midnight watering hole for *Gazette* staffers. (After that, the festivities moved up the hill to the Press Club in the basement of the Sheraton Hotel.)

The only difference between this day's announcement and any other was that Brodie asked me to send over the baseball writer to keep him company as soon as he woke up.

Before very long, the writer came to with a start, looked around, muttered a few profanities and announced that he'd better get to work on his story. I told him it had been done and that Brodie was waiting for him at Mother Martin's.

He seemed to think this was a fine idea and off he went. So much for trepidation about the standards of decorum at the *Gazette*.

• • •

It's hard to determine the point at which Ken Dryden appeared to lose his sense of humour and started taking life—and perhaps himself—a bit too seriously.

If you see him on TV now, he appears aloof and is invariably long-winded. But when he was playing for the Montreal Canadiens in the seventies, he was always available to the media. He was honest and often funny.

He was also notoriously cheap.

Hockey travel was much different in that era. The teams travelled on commercial flights and made their own way to the airport, at which point they checked in with the travelling secretary—if there was one. In the Canadiens' case, there was, but he also doubled as the coach. It was Scott Bowman who stood at one of the check-in counters with a stack of boarding passes that he handed out to the players and media as they showed up.

On the way into Montreal's Dorval Airport, about 400 yards from the terminal, was a Texaco gas station that allowed patrons to park for $1 a day. The airport parking, which was adjacent to the terminal, charged $2.

Dryden invariably parked at the gas station, a decision which, considering the vagaries of Montreal's weather, was not always wise.

The team had to catch its flight whether two feet of snow had just fallen or not, and Dryden's teammates took great pleasure in driving past him in their cars and honking their horns as they headed to the $2 parking while he trudged through knee-deep snow with his luggage over his shoulder and an extra dollar in his pocket.

• • •

Once the flight had been made and the players had arrived at their hotel, they often would meet in the lobby prior to going off to expensive restaurants. While they waited for stragglers, they frequently saw Dryden heading off for his dinner—up to his room with the bag of sandwiches he had just bought at the nearest Arby's.

I once suggested to Dryden that the reason he opted to play goal, as opposed to any other position, was that it provided him the opportunity to pick up the pennies that fans often threw at goaltenders in those days.

I suggested a lot of other inane things to him as well. He seemed to frequently lose a glove when he strayed from the net to handle the puck, and I opined that maybe he should get those idiot clips used by mothers to attach their children's mittens to their sleeves.

Dryden often took these smartass comments stoically, although he did occasionally deliver his own shot.

When Trac 2 razors were all the rage, for instance, Dryden looked down at my less-than-luxuriant Fu Manchu moustache, sneered and said, "What do you use to shave that thing? A Trac one-eighth razor?"

Sometimes, the shots escalated into a battle of wits and I rarely won.

When he came to Toronto as general manager of the Maple Leafs, he spent the first summer trying to decide whether Mike Murphy would or would not return as coach. This meant, of course, that hockey writers—not the most industrious group of people on the face of the earth—had to continuously take days out of their otherwise quiet summer to bring fans up to date on Dryden's latest non-decision.

The next year, he went through a similar process as he tried to decide on a general manager.

At one of the press conferences, I said, "Kenny, do you have something against hockey writers having the summer off?"

His response was instantaneous. "Believe me, Al, we have nothing against you taking a full-blown sabbatical."

One night, after the press box's supply of Häagen-Dazs ice cream was replaced by an inferior brand, I pointed out this switch to Dryden.

"I notice that since you arrived on the scene, Kenny, there has been deterioration in the quality of ice cream."

Again, Dryden's response was immediate.

"Well, Al, I'm sure deterioration of quality is a concept with which you are quite familiar."

• • •

Looking back on the Edmonton Oilers' first Stanley Cup, the one they won in 1984, it seemed to have been a relatively easy final series.

Of course, no Stanley Cup final is easy and perhaps if Oilers defenceman Kevin Lowe hadn't fired a verbal rocket at his teammates, it might not have turned out the way it did.

In the series opener on Long Island, the Oilers beat New York 1–0, but then lost 6–1 before heading home for the next two games.

The Oilers had been swept by the Islanders the year before, so when they won a game on the road, they were confident. Perhaps too confident.

"I remember when we got home and we were practising the next day," recalled Wayne Gretzky. "A few guys—and

I think I might have been one of them—are lah-di-dahing on the ice and having a good time. Andy Moog was another complainer, wondering why we needed to practise hard."

"Kevin Lowe went ballistic. He said, 'Listen, we're here to practise. The series is tied. It's 1–1. We're here to win the Cup. If you don't want to put in an hour's work, get off the ice right now.'

"I'll never forget he said that," said Gretzky. "I thought, 'You know, he's right,' and I think everybody else felt the same way. Right away, we all went up to another level."

And they won the next three games.

• • •

Even though NHL players have to wear the uniforms supplied by the team, there are no rules regarding underclothing. As a result, a lot of hockey players wear an undershirt to which they have developed an attachment.

Sometimes, thanks to the bizarre superstitions of athletes, they wear their favourite T-shirt long after it should have been retired. Invariably, these shirts have some sort of meaning for the player. They might promote a rock group, a bar, a sports drink, or once in a while, the player's annual golf tournament.

My favourite was the one that Chris Chelios was still wearing when he was playing in Detroit, long after his tenure with the Chicago Blackhawks had ended.

It had a picture of a police department shield and read, "Chicago Police Homicide. Our day starts when yours ends."

• • •

No one expects public-relations people who work for American teams to have intimate knowledge of Canadian geography. After all, they're Americans and invariably unfamiliar with anything outside their own borders.

Therefore, you can almost excuse the Tampa Bay Lightning when the team's official media guide said that goaltender Derek Wilkinson spent his summers in "his hometown of Belleville, Ontario, which is outside of Detroit, Michigan."

Belle River, Ontario, is on Lake St. Clair, which flows into the Detroit River, so even though the Tampa people are mistaken, you can understand the mix-up.

But there's no excuse for the San Jose Sharks who listed Patrick Marleau's birthplace as being "Aneroid, Saskatchewan, a suburb of Calgary."

If Calgary were anywhere close to the Saskatchewan border, this sort of mistake might be forgivable. But since Calgary is in south-central Alberta, it's inexcusable. In terms of distance, it's like saying Chicago is a suburb of Detroit.

● ● ●

Mike Craig was a free spirit who, to say the least, did not have the resolve to match his talent.

In his rookie season with the Minnesota North Stars in 1991, the team got as far as the Stanley Cup finals and lost to Mario Lemieux and the Pittsburgh Penguins. But as every hockey fan knows, the longer the playoffs last, the tougher they get. So Craig was a healthy scratch.

Sitting in the dressing room watching the game with the other black aces, Craig started to feel a bit peckish. He could hardly head out to one of the concession stands, so he called a local pizza outlet and ordered one of their specialties to be delivered to the players' entrance at the Met Center.

Not long afterwards, the pizza arrived and Craig went to the door, where an unforeseen problem arose. Craig had been riding the exercise bike in his underwear and had no money.

But he was nothing if not resourceful. "How about if I pay you with a signed Mike Modano hockey stick?" he asked.

The delivery boy thought that would be fine. Now it was just a matter of getting the stick.

The North Stars were in the dressing room for the second intermission, listening to coach Bob Gainey pointing out their deficiencies. The timing was perfect for Craig. He got one of Modano's sticks from the rack, took it over to get the autograph while Gainey talked, then took it out to the delivery boy.

It was an act of such irreverence that Craig became something of a folk hero among NHL players.

He lasted four seasons with the franchise and was then moved to the Toronto Maple Leafs, where he once again impressed his teammates. On this occasion, the ever-alert Craig was in mid-shift when he noticed that the Leafs had too many men on the ice. Something had to be done.

He quickly skated towards the bench and shouted, "Hey, we've got too many men on the ice. Get one off," and rejoined the play.

Until the whistle went for the penalty.

•   •   •

One of the worst trades in hockey history saw the Maple Leafs send Russ Courtnall to the Montreal Canadiens for John Kordic.

Courtnall was a fleet, offensive star, whereas Kordic was a dancing bear, a knuckle dragger who died in 1992 as a result of ingesting too many of the wrong chemical substances.

During Wayne Gretzky's barnstorming tour of Europe during the 1994 NHL lockout, Courtnall was yapping at Marty McSorley, ridiculing his play in the typical type of banter that goes on in dressing rooms all over the world.

But McSorley delivered a knockout blow.

"You know, Russ," he said loudly enough for everyone to hear, "even today, I'd still trade you even up for John Kordic."

THREE

Covering the Game before Twitter

Even though it was only for the briefest of periods, I have to admit that when I started in the newspaper business, Morse code was still used to transmit copy.

Granted, that method was dying out, but it was still used occasionally. If you worked for a small paper—or one of the afternoon papers that used to exist in that era—there might not be anybody in the office at night, so you couldn't call and dictate your story to a rewrite man. That had come to be the preferred method of transmission at the larger papers as long-distance telephone service became cheaper and more reliable.

Otherwise, you had to write your story in the press box or back at your hotel, then head for the nearest telegraph office, which was usually at the railroad station. You'd tell the attendant it was to be sent Press Rate Collect to your newspaper even though that wasn't really necessary because you'd typed the recipient's name at the top of each page as well. But that was the way we'd been told to do it, and if the story somehow went astray, you'd be asked if you did it that way, and if you didn't, you'd be in real trouble.

As recently as 1977, when I covered Team Canada's

exhibition games in Prague prior to the world championships in Vienna, the stories were sent by telegraph. On its best days, Czechoslovakia's phone service was terrible, and to make a call to Canada, you had to line up at the post office, fill out a form, hand it in and wait until some bureaucrat decided he was ready to place your call and send you to a little booth to pick up the antiquated handset.

Since the wait could be a long one and there was no guarantee the phone call wouldn't be cut off long before you were finished, it was faster and more reliable to let the telegraphers do it their way.

During the telegraph era in Montreal, the guy who transmitted the stories—and was older than dirt when I first met him in 1973—was Harry Brown. He had started at Canadian National not long after the First World War, and as a result, he knew all the hockey writers of the six-team era.

The Stanley Cup playoffs would draw veteran columnists and reporters from the other five NHL cities (Boston, Chicago, Detroit, New York and Toronto) and it must be said that these were not the kind of people who were known for their sobriety.

As their stories accumulated on his desk, Harry would dutifully massage his telegraph key and send them on their way.

Sometimes, at the end of the evening, it transpired that one (or more) of the writers had not filed any copy. Since he couldn't have filed it anywhere else, that meant only one thing. He was passed out drunk somewhere.

Accordingly, Harry would take a scrap from one of the stories he had transmitted, another scrap from a second, a bit more from a third and so on, until he had put together a complete story, which he then filed on behalf of the truant. It is said that in those days, no writer visiting Montreal ever missed a deadline.

• • •

Vyacheslav Kozlov had a long and productive career in the National Hockey League.

But it could have been longer and more productive.

Kozlov first arrived in North America for the World Junior Championship when it was held in Saskatoon during late 1990 and early 1991.

In those days, the Detroit Red Wings were bedevilling NHL president John Ziegler no end. The Soviet Union Ice Hockey Federation had worked out a deal to sell the rights to some of its players to the NHL—Igor Larionov, Sergei Makarov and Vladimir Krutov, for instance—and Ziegler had promised that in return for allowing these stars to join his league, he would prevent any further incidents of NHL poaching of Eastern European players. NHL teams, especially Detroit, had been chasing Soviet bloc players, sometimes successfully, for years.

The Wings operated by their own set of rules. They had orchestrated the defection of Petr Klima from Czechoslovakia, and they had convinced Sergei Fedorov to walk away from the 1990 Goodwill Games in Seattle and defect to the United States. Their next target was Kozlov. They had drafted him 45th overall the summer prior to the Saskatoon tournament, and accordingly, Red Wings assistant general manager Nick Polano went west to see what he could do to get Kozlov on board. The Wings had a chartered plane standing by on a rural airstrip, and Polano convinced Kozlov to come out of the hotel and join him in his rented SUV.

Kozlov loved the vehicle. In fact, he loved it so much that he asked if he could drive it. Polano said he certainly could. In fact, he could drive it to the waiting plane.

But Kozlov just stayed in the parking lot and drove around and around the hotel. He would like to join the Wings, he said, but he was worried about his family. Polano assured him that the Wings would take care of his family.

Kozlov was worried that the Soviets would get Ziegler to ban him from the NHL, but Polano knew the way the hockey world worked in those days. The Soviets would make a demand of that nature to Ziegler, but the Wings would offer a compensatory payment to the Soviets and they would take it.

Similarly, the NHL could, and probably would, fine the Wings $250,000. But owner Mike Ilitch would simply pay that as well. He looked upon these extra expenses as a cost of doing business.

Finally, Kozlov decided that despite Polano's urging, he wasn't ready to make the jump and went back into the hotel.

Had he accepted Polano's offer, he would probably not have gone back to the Soviet Union until years later when the regime changed. As it was, he went back with the junior team, and that summer was badly injured in a car accident that delayed the start of his full-time NHL career until 1993.

• • •

Under the rules of the NHL salary cap that came into being in 2005, an owner can't walk into a dressing room and offer cash incentives to his players. Bonuses of this nature count as salary and have to be declared before the season begins and registered with the league.

But that was not always the case.

When Bruce McNall owned the Los Angeles Kings, his team had moved into first place in the Smythe Division when McNall told the players that if they were still there at the end of the season, he'd give them a million dollars to divide among themselves.

Furthermore, he said, if the Kings went on to win the Stanley Cup, he'd plunk down another $1.5 million for the players to split.

NHL president John Ziegler was not at all happy about this. He pointed out to McNall the stipulations of league Bylaw 25.1.

Here's that bylaw, keeping in mind that the NHL, still struggling to emerge from the Middle Ages in so many ways, has obviously lost the battle when it comes to the correct use of capitalization:

"No Member Club, Club Official or representative of such club shall offer, or pay, or agree to pay to any of its players any bonus or reward which would be in effect a special inducement to win a game or series of games against any particular club or clubs."

So did McNall withdraw his offer to cough up $2.5 million in bonuses? He did not.

He simply referred Ziegler to Bylaw 25.3: "Any Club or Club Official violating the provisions of this By-Law shall be liable to a fine of Ten Thousand Dollars."

When you're willing to cough up $2.5 million, an extra ten grand (or Ten Grand) doesn't make much difference.

•   •   •

Life on the road invariably has its dull moments, especially on game days when, for a newspaperman, there's not a lot to do before the game begins in the evening.

But every so often, somebody livens up one of those game days with some memorable impromptu entertainment.

There was, for instance, the otherwise forgettable Saturday morning when Don Cherry and Gary Green staged a not-so-amicable mid-season chat in the lobby of the Westin Hotel in Edmonton.

Green, once a coach of the Washington Capitals and a long-time hockey announcer, had taken it upon himself to become a member of the Fair Play Commission, one of those bleeding-heart groups that pops up every so often to try to turn hockey into ballet. Needless to say, no one had asked Cherry to join the Fair Play Commission.

When the two encountered each other, Cherry, who is not known for suffering in silence, let it be known that he was sick of people "who live in Florida for most of the week, then come up here every so often to tell us how to run our sport."

Green was already angry at Cherry. He had seen the "Coach's Corner" segment on *Hockey Night in Canada* a couple of weeks earlier when Cherry had suggested that commission members were "at the trough" gobbling up taxpayers' dollars while plotting the emasculation of his game.

As the hockey hangers-on, who had just come back from the Oilers' morning skate, moved in to enjoy the show, Green threw gasoline on the fire by offering his unreserved opinion that fighting should be taken out of the game altogether.

Cherry said he could understand Green holding that view, "because you run all those hockey schools and that's what the mothers tell you to say."

Eventually, the debate over fighting became so heated that Cherry suggested it should be settled in a suitable manner—by the two stepping outside to have a fight.

Green, who is considerably shorter and lighter (and of course quieter) than Cherry, then decided that as far as he was concerned, the matter had gone far enough. As a gesture of conciliation, he put his hand on Cherry's shoulder while he made that point.

This was not the best of tactical moves. Cherry said that if the offending digits were not removed immediately, the fisticuffs would begin inside the hotel.

At that point referee Don Koharski, who had been among the crowd taking in the contretemps, used his professional training to separate the two and send them on their separate ways.

• • •

Tom McVie was a hockey lifer. His minor-league playing career took him to Toledo, Portland (twice), Dayton, Fort Wayne, Los Angeles, Seattle (twice), Phoenix and Johnstown.

As a coach, he worked in the National Hockey League, the Eastern Hockey League, the International Hockey League, the Central Hockey League, the World Hockey Association, the American Hockey League and the East Coast Hockey League.

One of his claims to fame, one that he was only too willing to demonstrate, was that after he had taken his dentures out, he could fit three hockey pucks into his mouth at once.

Another notable distinction, one of which he was less proud, was that when he was finally fired by the Winnipeg Jets after twenty-eight games of the 1980–81 season, the team's record stood at 1-20-7.

When he returned to the NHL as coach of the New Jersey Devils, he was only too aware that some of his previous coaching methods had not produced great success, so he was willing to be innovative.

When the Devils went into a slump, he felt it was because the players were not listening to his suggestions and were ignoring his game plans. He held a team meeting and told the players that since they didn't seem to think his strategy was worth following, they should devise their own. He told them to form committees and to work out their own penalty-killing and power-play methods.

"That way," he told them, "I can coach this team standing on my head."

The next day, the Devils were to leave town on a road trip. When they arrived at the check-in counter, McVie was waiting for them.

He was standing on his head.

• • •

In the 1989 playoffs, when the Vancouver Canucks were in the process of pushing the heavily favoured Calgary Flames to the limit and the seventh game was only minutes away, Vancouver coach Bob McCammon realized that a Knute Rockne speech would be counterproductive.

His team was so tight, McCammon figured, that a go-get-'em exhortation would only make matters worse.

Instead, to the rapt attention of his players, he told the story about a scientist who invented a machine that could raise or lower IQs. In the midst of an experiment, the phone rang and by the time the scientist returned to the machine, the subject's IQ had been lowered to five.

The scientist knew that he could correct the situation, but being a researcher, he was curious as to whether a man could function with an IQ of only five.

"Say something," he said.

The subject looked at him and said, "Go."

"Good start," said the scientist. "Say something else."

Again, the response was the same.

"Go."

"Come on," said the scientist. "I know your IQ is only five, but give it everything you've got. Sum up all your intellectual effort and say as much as you can."

The subject stared back, then screwed up his eyes, took a deep breath and said, "Go, Flames, go."

It would be nice to say that the Canucks won after that. But they didn't. They did come surprisingly close, however.

They had entered the series as heavy underdogs, and they took the seventh game to overtime. They even had a great chance to win when Stan Smyl had a breakaway, but he was stopped by Mike Vernon. Later, Vancouver's Petri Skriko fired a shot that Vernon didn't see, but it hit the post.

Finally, with a goal that would be illegal under today's rules, Joel Otto won it for Calgary, and the Flames went on to win the Stanley Cup.

●　●　●

Bob McCammon has long been one of the funniest men in hockey. He delights not only in wisecracks, but in recounting actual events. One of his favourites came during the Desert Storm offensive in the Gulf War.

McCammon was still coaching the Canucks at the time, and his enforcer was Gino Odjick—who is never likely to be seen on the *Jeopardy* Tournament of Champions. The Vancouver fans loved Odjick, and on this occasion, a couple of them put up a banner proclaiming, "Gino is tougher than Saddam."

From the bench, Odjick was able to see the sign, but it puzzled him. He turned to McCammon and asked, "Hey, Bob, what number is Saddam?"

Not long afterwards, the Canucks fired McCammon, perhaps for being unable to get his message through to people like Odjick.

• • •

McCammon didn't stay out of work long. The Edmonton Oilers hired him as a pro scout and then, as the 1994–95 season wound down, brought him in to provide some guidance for their new young coach, George Burnett.

Burnett was one of the few serious mistakes made by Oilers general manager Glen Sather. The Oilers had always been one of the most relaxed, laid-back teams in all sport. But no one had ever called Burnett relaxed or laid-back. He had been a good coach in junior hockey and may become a fine NHL coach someday. But Sather rushed him along too quickly and pushed him in over his head. In the NHL, it's difficult for coaches to gain respect at any time, but in that era, if you were thirty-two years old and had no previous NHL experience, it was virtually impossible.

The grim, humourless Burnett and the wry Bob McCammon were a study in contrasts. Burnett was fastidious about his appearance and paid close attention to detail, whereas the rumpled McCammon was a weathered veteran. Approaching the situation gingerly, McCammon asked what he could do to help. Burnett told him to watch the game from the press box and use the walkie-talkie to keep him apprised of tendencies.

McCammon had to suppress a grin. "Tendencies?" he asked.

"Tendencies," said Burnett.

So before long, McCammon made his call to the bench. "It's fourteen thousand, five hundred," he said to Burnett.

"What is?"

"The attendance is. Isn't that what you wanted from me?"

• • •

Harry Neale is another one of hockey's truly funny men. He had a long, varied coaching career in college, the World Hockey Association and then the NHL, before finally joining *Hockey Night in Canada* as one of the best colour men the show has ever had.

But he never coached or managed a championship team. The closest he came was with the 1981–82 Vancouver Canucks when he pulled off what he calls "the smartest move I ever made as a coach." That move was to get himself suspended for eight games for trying to punch a fan in Quebec City.

With Neale suspended, assistant coach Roger Neilson was forced to take control. Even though the suspension came late in the season, Neale could have resumed his coaching duties in the playoffs. Instead, he left Neilson in charge and under his guidance, the team went on a tear and made it all the way to the finals, where the New York Islanders knocked them out in four straight.

But as is always the case with coaches, the magic wears off, and less than two years later, Neale had to fire Neilson and go back behind the bench himself.

• • •

There are those who say Harry Neale's pre-game speeches were often hilarious, but certainly not suitable for repetition in polite company, and the players never knew what Neale might do next.

One night in St. Louis, he started his big line—Thomas Gradin, Stan Smyl and Curt Fraser—and they promptly allowed two goals. Over the years, Neale had got to know the off-duty cop who provided security at the visiting team's bench.

"Lend me your gun," he said.

"I can't do that, Harry," said the cop. "Get serious."

"Just for a minute," said Neale. "I'll give it right back."

Finally, despite misgivings, the cop acquiesced, and Neale walked behind his top line, now sitting on the bench. Holding the gun so the players could see it but the fans couldn't, Neale said, "If you guys don't smarten up, I'll shoot you before this game is over."

The Canucks rebounded and won the game.

• • •

By definition, great hockey players play the game better than anyone else. But experience has shown that they also know the game better than anyone else.

Prior to the 1998 Olympics in Nagano, Japan, the accepted wisdom was that four teams had a realistic opportunity to win the gold medal: Sweden, Russia, Canada and the United States. The others, it was agreed by most observers, had too many deficiencies in too many areas.

But Wayne Gretzky made a point that no one else had seemed to notice. The Czech Republic would have Dominik

Hasek in goal and that could negate a lot of any opponent's assets.

Gretzky added that, in his opinion, Hasek was the best player in the world—"better than Paul Kariya or Eric Lindros," he said in a reference to the two players widely conceded to be the NHL's best at the time.

Later, a casual conversation with Igor Larionov, concerning the outlook for the Olympics, led to the mention of what were seen as the top four teams.

"Don't forget the Czech Republic," warned Larionov.

"The Czech Republic? They don't have much."

"They've got Dominik Hasek," said Larionov. "Any time you've got Hasek, you've got a chance."

Sure enough, Hasek beat the Americans under coach Ron Wilson 4–1 in the elimination round to qualify for the semifinal.

Then he beat Canada in the semifinal. That was the game that featured the infamous shootout in which coach Marc Crawford left Gretzky on the bench and Hasek stopped all five Canadian shooters.

Then, to put a cap on a marvellous performance, he shut out Russia in a 1–0 game to win the gold medal for the Czech Republic, a result that was a shock to everyone—except Gretzky and Larionov.

● ● ●

At one time, a hockey writer was always identifiable by the portable typewriter that he carried with him almost everywhere.

For the electronic generation, I should probably explain that it looked like a box about 15 inches square and eight inches deep, with a handle on it. The typewriter itself was locked into the base of the carrying case so that it couldn't fall out, and the case's cover locked in place to give double security. At least, that was the theory.

One night, with the team bus due to depart for the Los Angeles airport in thirty seconds, *Montreal Gazette* columnist Tim Burke came running down the steps of the Great Western Forum only to have the case fly open and his typewriter fall out.

While the Canadiens sat in their bus and chuckled at his misfortune, Burke crawled around on hands and knees frantically picking up keys and letter pads that were rolling around on the steps.

Scotty Bowman made the bus wait, but when Burke climbed aboard, red-faced from both embarrassment and exertion, he was given a rousing ovation by the team.

• • •

The Canadiens had a rule that the staff sat in the back row on the team bus. The staff usually consisted of only coach Scotty Bowman and his assistant, Claude Ruel, but it occasionally included a team doctor and/or personnel director Al MacNeil. The reporters sat in the two rows in front of them.

On most teams, the coach likes to sit at the front, but Bowman preferred the back for two reasons. First, the players never knew when he was watching them and were therefore less likely to get up to mischief. Second, he carried a tiny portable radio that worked better in the back seat than the front. He liked to keep track of what was going on elsewhere in the NHL, and if he could find out the other scores around the league, he'd keep us up to date.

But it wasn't just hockey that grabbed Bowman's attention. In October, he'd listen to the World Series and let us know what was going on there as well. When most people were watching Reggie Jackson earn the title "Mr. October," we were hearing about his exploits from Scott Bowman.

• • •

After a game, the Montreal players would put their carry-on bags into the overhead luggage rack, but if the bus was just going to or from the rink for the morning skate, that rack was empty—unless one of the reporters put his portable typewriter up there.

That's exactly what *Gazette* reporter Bob Morrissey did one day. This was not a problem until the bus driver had to hit the brakes suddenly while going downhill.

Unimpeded by other luggage, the typewriter skidded madly down the rack for the entire length of the bus, reached the front, hit the low retaining barrier, careened over it and landed with a crash in the bus's stairwell. En route, it narrowly missed the head of six-foot-four Pete Mahovlich, who was sitting in the front seat.

Pete was not amused and let Morrissey know about it, especially since he occasionally stood in the stairwell instead of sitting in his seat. He could have subsequently switched to a less dangerous seat, but he didn't want to do that. Like most hockey players, he was a creature of habit and he viewed that front-right seat as his birthright.

Instead, for every trip after that, every reporter boarding the bus carrying his portable typewriter had to listen to Pete warn him of the dangers of putting it into the luggage rack.

• • •

Ken Dryden's term as general manager of the Toronto Maple Leafs was not the highlight of his career.

He made—or allowed his associate Mike Smith to make—some awful trades. He got his wrist slapped by the league for trying to lure Bob Gainey away from the Montreal Canadiens, and most importantly, he failed miserably in his attempt to return the team to its long-forgotten glory days.

Nevertheless, he took himself far too seriously, never a good idea when people like Glen Sather travel in general-managerial circles.

Sather has always been a troublemaker, one of those guys who loves to needle people, especially those who, like Dryden, have a high opinion of themselves. That was true even back in the seventies when both Dryden and Sather played for the Montreal Canadiens.

In those days, Sather seemed to spend most of his time thinking of ways to annoy Dryden, and he loved doing it in public—usually in an airport while the team was enduring one of its many waits for a commercial flight.

One day Sather announced that many people, especially goaltenders, didn't have very good reflexes. To demonstrate this, he challenged Dryden to take a simple test.

Clearly, Dryden knew better. He made it clear that he wanted no part of Sather's latest game. But with all his team-mates urging him on, he finally acceded to peer pressure.

"Oh, all right, Glen," he said. (At that time, Dryden was the only person on the team who didn't use Sather's universal nickname of "Slats"). "If it amuses you, we'll do it."

Dryden had to extend his hand with his thumb and forefinger about 2 inches apart. Sather held a crisp new dollar bill vertically between them. Then he let the dollar drop. It was his contention that Dryden's reflexes weren't good enough to grasp the dollar before it fell to the floor.

They weren't.

This occasioned much merriment from the other players, as Sather shook his head in mock pity. What a shame it was that Dryden couldn't do better, that he had a career as a professional athlete but his reflexes were so poor.

Of course, the fact is that no human being has reflexes that will act at that speed. Naturally enough, Dryden challenged Sather to do it, but by then, Sather had found more pressing matters to attend to.

•   •   •

Another day. Another airport. Same cast.

In Sather's mouth was a contraption that looked like a tiny pipe. Attached to it was little a wire hoop with a net under it. As he wandered around the waiting area, Sather would casually blow into the pipe. This pushed up a little ball, which would drop through the hoop and into the net.

Dryden was busy reading a paper someone had discarded, but Sather walked back and forth in front of him blowing the ball up into the air and dropping it through the hoop. Finally, Dryden had had enough.

"Small things amuse small minds, Glen," he said.

This was the opening Sather had been waiting for. "I bet you can't do it," he said.

"I'm sure if you can do it, Glen, I can do it."

"Well, I'll bet you a dollar you can't. Here, give it a try."

Once again, the crowd of teammates had gathered. Dryden blew into the pipe. Up went the ball. Down came the ball—onto the floor.

"That'll be a dollar," smirked Sather, while the other Canadiens hooted in glee.

What he hadn't told Dryden, of course, was that he had been practicing for hours. His performance was nowhere near as easy as he had made it look.

• • •

By 1998, Dryden was the general manager of the Maple Leafs, and Sather was the general manager of the Edmonton Oilers.

This was an era when the Oilers were financially weak, and there had been some suggestions that a pre-season tournament involving Canadian teams might liven up, and increase the profitability of, those typically boring exhibition games that teams stage prior to the season.

It was still ten months before the proposed tournament, but talks had begun; I asked Sather how they were progressing. He said the deal had been done until Dryden pulled out.

"He has forgotten about when he was kissing everybody's butt last year so he could switch conferences," Sather said. "We supported him and now he has forgotten that he's a Canadian."

Since he made this statement while the Oilers and Leafs were playing a game in Maple Leaf Gardens, it was an easy matter to wander down to the other end of the press box and ask Dryden about this.

Because I know Sather well, I probably should have known better. For that matter, so should Dryden.

He immediately became visibly angry, growling through tight lips that the charge was not only outrageous, it was totally incorrect.

He took a deep breath to compose himself then said,

"We have spent more time thinking about this tournament, working on this tournament than Mr. Sather—including a conference call yesterday which I was a part of, Calgary was a part of, Ottawa was a part of and Montreal was a part of.

"And noticeable by their absence was Edmonton. And it was a long discussion about this tournament."

By now, it was clear to me—but not to Dryden evidently—that this was another one of Sather's little games with Dryden as the target. But since a good column was brewing, I went along with it. I asked why Edmonton would not have been involved in the discussion.

"Now, isn't that interesting?" asked Dryden, his voice dripping sarcasm. "That might be a good question for you and your friend who always has an axe to grind."

Back to the other end of the press box. Why hadn't Sather participated in the call?

"I couldn't stand listening to him for an hour," he said.

But would the tournament take place anyway?

"Kenny is backing out," insisted Sather. "He has forgotten his roots. The only reason we got a game against them last year was that [Leafs owner] Steve Stavro is a good Canadian."

Back to Dryden's end of the press box.

"It is completely unfair and inappropriate," he said when told of Sather's charges. "I'm mad at axes to grind and idiot questions like this. What fool would ever say such a thing? It's outrageous and it's wrong."

To answer Dryden's question, it was Sather who had said it.

"Yes," said Dryden. "Slats is wonderful at dropping little balloons. Then who's the first to disappear? Slats. Everybody else is working on it, talking about it, and [Sather] who is the hero of every story he tells, including this one, was here watching the practice yesterday when the rest of us were here working on a conference call."

Sather, he pointed out, enjoys stirring up trouble by making public statements intended to shock. Not much argument there.

"And how often has Slats been right?" Dryden asked. "Not very often.

"Glen Sather is in a world that is about this big," said Dryden, using his hands to follow the contours of his body, "and does not go beyond the boundaries of the skin of Glen Sather.

"Everything is his version of the world. It happens to be, in most cases, very wrong, but there are certain people who don't think so.

"Who knows whether we're going to have this tournament? But at least we are working on it."

Back to the other end to let Sather know that this time, he might have overstepped the bounds. Dryden was genuinely angry.

"I don't care," said Sather. "Kenny lives in his own little world and anything that doesn't fit into his world, he doesn't like."

That charge sounded familiar. It was exactly what Dryden had said about Sather.

"The only way to get him to do anything is to make him angry."

Unfortunately for hockey fans, they made each other angry. The tournament would have been a good idea, but with the level of animosity being what it was, it never came about.

FOUR

The glamorous life of the sportswriter

For several years, the Toronto Maple Leafs travelled to Philadelphia for an afternoon game during the American Thanksgiving break.

In 1998, the game was played on a Friday afternoon, and in the evening many of the Philadelphia players were planning to attend a concert by an up-and-coming Canadian rock group.

Tim Wharnsby and I were both covering the game for the *Toronto Sun*, and Tim was a good friend of Chris Gratton, who was playing for the Flyers at the time. "You guys should come to this concert tonight," said Gratton. "Just tell them at the door you're with the Flyers." Then, because he was accustomed to dealing with sportswriters, he added, "It won't cost you anything."

It was far from a headline event. The gig was held in an old movie theatre that had had its seats torn out. There might have been three hundred people there, but probably not.

We were all standing around the balcony area in midshow when a security guard decided that Wharnsby and I had to go downstairs because only the Flyers were allowed on the balcony.

We explained that we had been invited by one of the Flyers and should therefore stay, but using logic on a security guard is like showing up early for a doctor's appointment: you're free to try it, but it won't do you any good. It didn't matter much. We went downstairs to stand on the sloping floor and enjoyed the rest of the concert. Then we went backstage to chat with the group.

It turned out that the lead singer watched *Hockey Night in Canada* whenever he could and was a big hockey fan. In fact, his godfather was Harry Sinden. He wanted some tips for the group's hockey pool, so we tried to offer a few insights. We all got along well, and he suggested that when the group played in Toronto in about three months, we attend as his guests.

That event was a bit bigger. It was opening night at the Air Canada Centre. The attendance was 17,500. The singer was Gord Downie, and the group was the Tragically Hip.

If they played in Philadelphia now, they'd need a much larger venue than an old movie house.

• • •

During my early days at the *Globe and Mail*, where it was career enhancing to be opposed to hockey violence, I would occasionally fill a quiet day with a column announcing the latest Team Cement Head.

Determining who qualified for the team was fairly straightforward. It involved a simple ratio of a player's penalty minutes to the number of points he had racked up. Colin Campbell, now the guy in charge of NHL discipline, had one point versus 89 penalty minutes, a ratio that earned him a spot on the team.

Through the media grapevine, he sent a message that he was furious and that he intended to confront me the next time I attended a Canucks game.

I wasn't too happy about this. Even the most out-of-shape NHL player was in a lot better condition than me, and I was at the other end of the toughness spectrum from any guy on Team Cement Head.

Still, you can't let yourself be intimidated, so when there were a lot of other people around to provide witnesses to an assault charge, I went over to Campbell.

"I've got a problem with you putting me on Team Cement Head," he said with a glare.

Awaiting some sort of onslaught, either physical or verbal, I told him I was aware of that. "A lot of my penalty minutes were misconducts. I don't think you should use those in your rankings."

That was the end of it. Campbell laughed. The anger and the threatened recriminations had all been part of another one of his jokes.

●　　●　　●

When Campbell was coach of the New York Rangers from 1995 to 1998, the game was often dismal, but nobody in the media wanted to miss the post-game press conference, which was invariably entertaining.

There was, for instance, the time when Rangers all-star defenceman Brian Leetch got smashed against the boards and went down in a heap. The media wanted to know what Campbell first thought about when he saw that.

"My job," he said.

That kind of irreverence has always been there. One day,

the subject of honouring players came up, and it was noted that even though a lot of sweater numbers get retired, the fans seem to love it. Campbell had other ideas.

"I don't see what the big fuss is about retiring sweaters," he said. "I had my sweater retired three times."

"You did?"

"Sure. Of course, I was in it every time."

• • •

Around the mid-seventies, hockey writers started sending stories by fax. This was quite the novelty at the time and because the technology was in its infancy, the process was a lot more complex than it is today.

But now, you didn't have to rush off to a telegraph office. In each NHL press box was an employee of the company that provided the fax service—Canfax in the case of the three Canadian teams.

Each sheet had to be individually attached to a drum, then a cover was lowered and the recipient's phone number was dialed. A series of whines and squeals signalled the readiness of the machine at the other end. The start button was pressed; the drum began to turn (assuming all was working well, which wasn't always the case), and soon, the drum was rotating rapidly. As it did so, a little indicator needle moved along to show how much of the sheet had been transmitted.

Each page took about four minutes to send, and each hockey story required about four pages. Time was too tight after a game to allow a reporter to wait until his entire story had been written and then spend another quarter of an hour transmitting, so each page was sent off upon completion.

You'd pull the finished page out of your typewriter,

scream "FAX" at the top of your lungs and wait for the fax attendant, usually a high-school kid, to come running up to take your copy and run back to his fax machine at the end of the press box.

These kids were invariably good at their job and if their machine was clear, they would occasionally hover around waiting for a customer to finish typing a page. Unfortunately for them, the writer, caught up in his own thoughts, might not notice their presence and scream "FAX" into the ear of a kid who was already reaching over his shoulder for the finished sheet.

It was not an easy way to write a story. You were usually under a tight deadline and feverishly banging in quotes you'd hastily scribbled in your notebook. If you were typing your third page, you couldn't go back to your first or second page and check to see if you'd already used a specific quote, or made reference to a certain aspect of the game.

Eventually, Canfax was phased out of the press box when faxing was superseded by other forms of transmission. But in Toronto, it left behind a lasting impact.

The usual Canfax kid in Maple Leaf Gardens was Gord Stellick, who, because he worked cheaply, was hired by Harold Ballard to do odd jobs for the Leafs. By 1988, Stellick had risen steadily in the Leafs organization to the point that Ballard made him the general manager.

•   •   •

The next technological "advance" after the fax machine was a Teleram. This was a 35-pound early computer the size of a suitcase with a baby-blue imitation-leather cover. We had to lug this monstrosity around from town to town and routinely staggered through airports, arms aching from the Teleram in one hand and the luggage for a ten-day road trip in the other.

In those days, there was no such thing as a wheeled suitcase. Even those little folding luggage carts that predated wheeled suitcases hadn't yet made the scene. You could use a bag with a shoulder strap, but that just meant that your shoulder hurt instead of your arm. And you usually had to take a lot of the weight with your arm anyway to prevent the bag strap from sliding off your shoulder.

The cover of the Teleram lifted off to reveal a boxlike contraption with a keyboard protruding from the front. On the vertical face of the main body was a port into which you inserted a specially formatted cassette tape. In theory, there were 60 blocs on the tape, each one capable of holding about three hundred words.

There was also a tiny screen, not much bigger than one found today on a BlackBerry, and as you typed, the letters came up on the screen.

There were several problems with these machines. The first was that the usual game story was around eight hundred words, so you had to create three blocks of copy to file a single story. Another was that although there was space on the tape for 60 blocs, numbers 1–50 didn't work.

Once you had your 250 to 300 words for a bloc, you stored it. The catch was that if by chance you wrote too much copy for the bloc to handle, the entire bloc disappeared.

Forever.

To get the thing to transmit, you had to plug it into a phone line. That meant, of course, that the phone had to be unplugged from the jack. Then you typed in the number you were transmitting to, and when (if) it connected, you called up the number of each bloc, one by one.

It was possible that for some reason you might want to hang on to a feature story you'd written earlier. But let's say it was on blocs 52, 55 and 57. You'd write your game story on blocs 51, 53 and 56. Then you'd send your story to the office, unhook the machine from the phone jack, reconnect the telephone and call the office to make sure they received it. That's when they'd say, "We got two legs, but the other one was part of that drivel you wrote last week."

So you'd have to go through the whole process again of hooking up the machine to the phone line, dialing up, etc., etc.

Fortunately, the era of the prototype Teleram did not last very long. It did have one upside however.

Because it was so cumbersome and because it was too fragile to be turned over to an airline's baggage-smashers, it had to be taken with you as carry-on luggage. Some airline check-in attendants balked at this—unless you flew first class.

Unfortunately for the *Globe and Mail's* accountants, I encountered balky attendants at pretty well every check-in desk. That was certainly my story at the time, and I'm sticking to it.

●   ●   ●

Next came the new generation of Teleram—the Portabubble. The major difference between this machine and its predecessor was that the Portabubble usually worked.

It was a smaller and lighter version of the Teleram, but with a larger screen.

It also had its own memory, so there was no need for cassette tapes.

Most of the time, it was easier to transmit using this machine. On the top of the machine were two rubber-rimmed couplers, one for each end of a telephone handset. You didn't have to plug the machine into a phone jack. You just made the call and shoved the handset into the appropriate receptacle.

There was, however, an occasional problem. (Surely you knew this was coming.) The machine communicated by transmitting sound waves. If you were sending an off-day story from a nice quiet hotel room, all was well.

But if you were trying to send your column in the dying moments of a close hockey game in a place like Chicago Stadium, you were in trouble.

For a hockey columnist, the deadlines worked this way. You wrote a column during the game that had to be in no later than the end of the game. After the game, you rewrote it, either partially or in its entirety.

In an overtime game, a close game or a game taking place in a different time zone, you could file most of the column in the dying moments, then file the top of the column—with the final score—as soon as the game ended. That latter filing was often just the lead paragraph or two, so it could be dictated. But because of deadline restrictions, the rest of the column had to be in the copy editor's hands before that so that it could get into the first edition on time.

The difficulty with the Portabubble was that it picked up crowd noises, which garbled transmission. So you had to shove the telephone handset as far into the coupler as it would go, pick up the entire machine, hold it to your stomach as tightly as you could, bend over so that your body was below the level of the press-box work area and pray that you'd blocked out enough crowd noise to allow the coupler to hear the machine's transmission and nothing else.

Now you know why most veteran sportswriters are overweight. The bigger the stomach, the better the chance of getting the Portabubble to work in a noisy arena.

•   •   •

The Portabubble was eventually replaced by the TRS-80, a cheap, sturdy Radio Shack machine that—despite often being referred to by its users as a "Trash-80"—worked well under most conditions.

It didn't have much storage capacity by today's standards, but it had a lot more than its predecessors.

Again, crowd noise created a transmission problem, but the TRS-80 had couplers that were attached to the machine by a cord. That way, only the couplers had to be enveloped by your stomach, not the entire machine.

After that, the advances were fast and furious. Colour screens came in and they produced images, not just words. Storage capacity was phenomenal and the transmissions were instantaneous and unaffected by noise. In most arenas now, the team provides a Wi-Fi signal, so the writer no longer needs to worry about access to a telephone. Nor does he or she need jacks, couplers, extension wires or any of the other accoutrements that were once mandatory.

You could even play games on these machines, and I know of at least one sportswriter who whiled away countless hours of what would otherwise have been Leafs-induced tedium by playing every known scenario of Railroad Tycoon at every level and in every generation.

I won't say who he was, but if you know a strategy that works to get cement to the ports in the Antarctica scenario, drop me a line.

• • •

From 1978 until his death in 2007, Tom Johnson never spoke to me. It had to do with an incident that took place during the 1978 playoffs. At that time, the Boston Bruins were considering getting rid of Don Cherry as their coach (which they did shortly afterwards anyway, so that should tell you something about the power of the press).

I was covering hockey for the *Montreal Gazette* and I wrote that if anyone were to be axed from the Bruins' hierarchy, that someone should not be Cherry.

I said that the primary person to blame for the problems affecting the Bruins was GM Harry Sinden, who had been in over his head ever since he left the Whitby Dunlops. I went on to say that in fairness, it had to be conceded that assistant GM Tom Johnson did not deserve even the most minuscule amount of blame, because in all his years with the team, he had never been known to do anything at all.

I insisted that Cherry deserved to stay on, if necessary at the expense of both Sinden and Johnson.

Cherry had seen a copy of the column at the hotel and, when the team bus arrived at the Montreal Forum, went to a nearby *Gazette* box, stuffed in three dollars and grabbed every paper in the stack. Then he went to the dressing room and handed out the sports sections to the Boston players. One of them tore out a copy of the column and put it on the bulletin board.

Shortly afterwards, Johnson came in, read the column and, without a word, ripped it off the board.

I presume he didn't like it, but he never actually told me so. For the next twenty years, he glared at me every time our paths crossed. But he never said a word. And as near as I could figure out, he never did anything for the Bruins either.

•   •   •

It's safe to say that I was not John Ziegler's favourite sportswriter.

For most of his tenure, I was relentlessly critical of the way he ran the league: poor decisions regarding American network-television coverage; his penny-wise, pound-foolish decisions on every aspect of the game; his inability to understand the basics of media relations; his inability to help the league grow in the United States, and so on.

Therefore, it was understandable that he not only snubbed me in person and ignored my phone calls, but would go to great lengths to avoid my questions during press conferences. Understandable or not, it's not good public relations. I've been critical of Ziegler's successor, Gary Bettman, as well, but Bettman is sharp enough to know that if he loses his composure at a press conference, he's the one who looks bad, not the person who asked the question.

When Ziegler was president from 1977 to 1992, hockey's media contingent was not only a relatively small group, it was fairly insular. All the members knew one another and for the most part, they were friends.

Everyone knew that Ziegler could be counted upon to blow his stack and therefore, in the hope of livening up an otherwise dull press conference, they did what they could to encourage him to do so.

For the first ten years of Ziegler's regime, there was some sniping between us, and there were some cool relations. But it was not until December 1987 that the serious confrontations began.

On that occasion, the league's governors were holding their annual meeting in Palm Beach, Florida, and by mid-afternoon of the first day, I was the only media representative in attendance.

As a result, Ziegler decided that a lifetime of tradition could be scrapped on the spot. Instead of the league's president giving a press conference at the end of each day's proceedings—as had been the case as long as anybody could remember—Ziegler decreed that there would be only one press briefing and it would come at the meeting's conclusion, three days hence.

No doubt, he was quite pleased with himself for pulling off this little coup. The *Globe and Mail* had gone to considerable expense to send me to Florida, and now the only news they'd get would be what I could scrape up from the individual governors. Furthermore, without his briefing, I'd have to start from scratch, not knowing what had been on the agenda.

However, a few minutes after I'd been informed of Ziegler's decision, a reporter from the Associated Press arrived. Then another one from United Press International showed up. Ziegler's ploy had backfired.

Even Ziegler knew that it was to his benefit to get maximum publicity for the NHL, but now he had to tell the two big American wire services that they could cool their heels for three days. He also knew that even though it would mean my doing a lot more work—not a prospect that appealed to me—I'd eventually find out most of what was happening. But these guys wouldn't.

Suddenly, Ziegler started backtracking. His edict to scrap end-of-day press conferences would stand, he said, but he would hold end-of-day briefings as long as he was not asked about ongoing issues.

What a fiasco.

Every issue the NHL governors discuss is ongoing. Even if they decide to shut down a team, for instance, there's still the ongoing issue of what happens to the players. So Ziegler would answer some questions in nebulous fashion, then decide he couldn't answer a follow-up to clarify the situation—especially if it came from me—because it related to an ongoing issue.

After a few minutes of this, I suggested that perhaps the league still had some way to go with regard to another ongoing issue: media relations. This started him spluttering and shouting and turning red.

But since he had been withholding all the good stuff regarding the governors' deliberations, he had made sure that the wire-service guys had no real news to report. As a result, they contented themselves with reporting on his tantrum.

• • •

On another occasion, in front of a full media contingent in Montreal, Ziegler studiously ignored my attempts to ask a question. I stood patiently with my hand up, but he always acknowledged someone else, and he was particularly prompt to curry the favour of the New York media.

So Mark Everson of the *New York Post* put up his hand

and, when Ziegler acknowledged him, said, "I think Al Strachan is trying to ask a question."

There was much laughter, none of it from Ziegler.

• • •

At other times, people would simply not raise their hands, leaving Ziegler with no choice but to acknowledge me. All the hockey writers seemed to enjoy these confrontations, and in the bar at night, we'd laugh about them. However, Ziegler's assistants told me that the disputes rattled him considerably and that he wouldn't be worth living with for the rest of the day, snapping at everyone who came within range.

But he never seemed to learn. The last explosion came during the June 1991 draft in Buffalo when he once again decided to withhold as much information as possible. He said that he thought it was a good idea to limit discussion on some matters.

"And keep the fans in the dark," I announced in a stage whisper. That did it. He lost his composure again, turned various shades of red and started shouting about lies and distortions.

Since he was offering no information that was remotely newsworthy, the three local TV people jumped all over this performance.

There, on the 11 o'clock news on three channels, was the NHL president making one of his remarkably rare trips to Buffalo, and in the process making a fool of himself.

That evening, a group of us were at *Buffalo News* hockey writer Jim Kelley's house having a party. When the sports news came on TV, we all laughed uproariously—partly at Ziegler's performance and partly at the fact that two of the TV people got my name wrong and the third made no attempt at identifying me. None of the viewers would know or care about who I was, but they did know that the man who was supposed to be running the National Hockey League, and who was supposed to be a top-level executive, was acting like a spoiled child in a playground dispute.

•   •   •

Ziegler never did figure out how to handle the media, from the day he became president in 1977 until the day he left the league in what was purported to be a resignation in 1992.

He was such an easy target that it was never difficult to get though a slow day by writing a column carving him. Eventually, he demanded a meeting with the *Globe and Mail.* The catch was, he said, that he was so incensed at my behaviour that he couldn't trust himself to remain under control. So instead of presenting his case himself, he was sending some lackeys.

What a great admission that was. Here was a man who was supposed to be running a multimillion-dollar league and working with some of the continent's top business people, but he couldn't control his emotions in a meeting being held to discuss what I had written about him. I wasn't even going to be there in person.

So in came NHL vice-president Brian O'Neill, league spin doctor Bill Wilkerson and a third flunkey. The *Globe's* brass patiently listened to all their complaints.

The one charge that was well founded, they decided, was that I had done a program piece for the Calgary Flames that was full of praise for certain developments in the NHL over the years.

The NHL's point was that if I wrote a glowing article for a program, why couldn't I write in a similar vein in the

Globe and Mail? As it happened, every example cited in the program piece had been used in the *Globe* at one time or another—but not all lumped together in one article.

The result was not the one the league wanted. I was banned from writing program articles for NHL teams, since the newspaper decided it constituted a conflict of interest. However, that was their only censure. As for my approach to Ziegler and the league, they admitted that they had previously been harbouring some slight concerns that I might have been too harsh. After meeting the league executives in person, however, they were surprised I had been so restrained.

"These guys are even worse than you say," laughed the managing editor. "Keep up the good work."

•   •   •

One night when Bob Berry was the coach of the Canadiens, we decided to head over to Montreal's famous Crescent Street for the evening.

Quebec had video-gaming machines in those days, but they were supposed to be for amusement only. You put your money into the machine, just like today's gaming machines, but you didn't get any money back. You simply racked up points.

But this being Montreal, the rules were, of course, stretched to the limit. In fact, they were broken. The bar owners, at least the ones on Crescent Street, would keep track of the points won by their regulars and convert them into free drinks.

When he'd finished playing, the patron would call over the bar manager who would enter the number of points the player had won in a large book, then clear the machine.

Berry and I were much more interested in providing the

bar with a more traditional form of bar business, but there was a machine nearby and because it was something of a novelty, when the owner came over to pay his regards, we asked him about it.

He explained the procedure and showed us the book in which he kept his tabulations.

There, prominent on the list of patrons who were owed a large number of drinks, was one of Berry's players.

"Look at that," said Berry. "That guy shouldn't be coming in here and playing gambling machines. That's got to be against the league rules. It's definitely against my rules."

"But he's got all these points," said the bar owner.

"Don't worry about that," said Berry. "We'll take care of them for him."

There was no bill that night.

• • •

No one ever suggested that Bob Murdoch should be on an all-star team.

But at the same time, no one ever suggested that he was anything less than an honest player, one of the many of that breed in the NHL who play hard, care about the game and always do their best.

He spent eleven seasons in the NHL, most of them with the Los Angeles Kings in an era when they were little more than one of the league's afterthoughts, and went on to coach both the Chicago Blackhawks and Winnipeg Jets. After he suffered the fate that all NHL coaches suffer, he headed to Europe to coach.

Hockey is a lot like malaria. Once it's in your blood, you've got it for life.

Murdoch even coached Italy, not one of the world's hockey powers, in the 1998 Nagano Olympics. Out of all this, he has one memory that overrides all the others:

"When Gordie Howe played his final year—when he was fifty-one years of age—for Hartford, I played against him," recalled Murdoch.

"We went into the corner and I still remember it. He elbowed me in the head. I didn't wash my face for a week.

"And you know what I'll always remember? When I'm sitting on the balcony of my cottage when I'm seventy-five and we're having a glass of wine with my grandchildren and my wife, and we're talking, I'll tell them about Gordie Howe elbowing me in the head."

FIVE

Don

I first met Don Cherry in the early 1970s. He was coaching the Boston Bruins. I was working for the *Montreal Gazette*.

And with the Bruins-Canadiens rivalry being what it was, Don was a godsend. Few people in the world can transform an already acrimonious situation into open warfare quite as well—or quite as quickly—as Don.

Because newspaper people are happiest when people are at each other's throats, Don's arrival behind the Boston bench was cause for a media celebration.

As Gordon Burns put it so well in his book *Fullalove*, "I knew that on newspapers, the universal motto, although nobody might ever admit it, was: The worse it gets, the better I like it."

Over the next decade, Don and I remained friends. I travelled a lot covering hockey, having moved to the *Globe and Mail* in 1980, and he was working for *Hockey Night in Canada*. We'd run into each other here and there and, as he would put it, "have a couple of pops."

In those days, he wasn't quite the prisoner of his own notoriety that he is now. It has been decades since he was able to go into a bar without being mobbed. He can't even get through an airport. He'll show up more than an hour before his flight, intending to spend some time in the lounge, only to find himself still signing autographs and posing for pictures when it's time to go to the gate.

As a result, when he's on the road with *Hockey Night in Canada*, he leaves some beers on ice in his hotel room when he goes to the game. Afterwards, he and Ron MacLean head back to Don's room and wind down in private. Don would love to go with the media guys on off-nights, but he knows he wouldn't be able to enjoy himself, so he just stays in his room.

We thought we had the problem solved one night in Edmonton during the Oilers' dynasty.

We all went to the same pub every night, it being near the hotel and we being creatures of habit, but it was closed on Sundays. But on one Sunday when the Oilers weren't playing, the owner said he would open up just for the media regulars. No one else would be allowed in.

We told Don about this and he came along, thinking he could have a peaceful night in a pub with friends.

But it was not to be. The owner's wife was there as well, and she pestered Don so mercilessly that he went back to the hotel.

•   •   •

On a couple of occasions, Don let me use his cottage on Wolfe Island (a beautiful locale at the western end of the Thousand Islands close to the Ontario–New York State border) for a family vacation. He placed only one condition on my stay. I was to deliver verbal abuse to any American bass fishermen who came too close to the shore. It was Don's opinion that

Americans fishing for bass off Wolfe Island should do so in American waters, not on the Canadian side.

We discovered that we had a mutual interest in British naval history, and Don would often suggest that we spend some time in England together visiting the country's historical sites.

I, in turn, would pass this sentiment along to my wife, Marian, who would pass along her own sentiment: "You're not going to England without me."

I could understand her feelings. We went to England every summer and both of us loved it there. Naturally, if I was going, she wanted to go along. Don, however, didn't see our proposed tour as a family outing.

In August 1988, we were all at Wayne Gretzky's wedding in Edmonton. Don came over to us and said to Marian, "Why won't you let Al go to England with me?"

It must be said that Don Cherry in full bluster is an intimidating sight. He's physically large; he's famous; and he has had lots of practice at imposing his will upon others.

Like many people who have found themselves backed into a corner by Don, Marian capitulated.

"He can go if he wants," she said.

We went the next month.

•   •   •

To Marian's credit, she did a lot of research—in the pre-Internet era when research wasn't quite so easy—to help us make sure we didn't go to places that had shut down or that were in the midst of renovation.

I went over a couple of days early, then, on the appointed day, met Don at London's Heathrow Airport. (A life of

travelling with hockey teams where others make all the
arrangements has left him incapable of finding his own way
from the airport to downtown.)

We dropped off his luggage at the hotel and went right
to St. Paul's Cathedral where the remains of Lord Horatio
Nelson lie pickled in the basement. Don was enthralled. To
be so close to history in such a magnificent building was the
perfect beginning to the trip.

Over the course of the next week, we strolled around
London visiting various notable spots, such as the British
Museum and the Tower of London. We took a boat down the
river Thames to Greenwich to visit the *Cutty Sark* and the
National Maritime Museum. We took a train to Portsmouth
to see three great ships of British naval history: the *Victory*,
the *Mary Rose* and the *Warrior*. We went to a couple of Gilbert
and Sullivan productions. We went to more than one pub.

All in all, Don said that with apologies to his wife, Rose,
it was the best week of his life. The honeymoon was great,
but...

• • •

Don Cherry visits the Tower of London:

The famous British crown jewels are on display here, so
there can be lengthy lineups, but on the day we went, we
didn't have to wait very long before we were allowed to enter
the room. Viewings are regimented. Once inside, you are
channelled up to the large, circular glass display case that
holds the priceless historical items. You walk around the case,
and then you're channelled out of the room again.

On a raised platform behind you are guards.

Directly in front of Don and me were some German

tourists who were clearly excited at being so close to such valuable historical artifacts. They were talking loudly to each other in German and pointing to various aspects of the display.

Don turned to the guard who was standing above us and said, "They're probably talking about how close they came to having these things," he said.

The guard laughed. "They didn't come that close, mate," he said.

• • •

In September 2007, Don and I met by chance in the departure lounge at Heathrow.

Don was with his son Tim, and they'd just come back from visiting the battlefields of France, where some of their family members had fought during the First World War.

I had been visiting my own son, Andrew, who lives in London.

We had plenty of time to kill before our flights, and once we'd solved a few of the world's problems (they're all caused by liberals), the conversation turned to the concept of a book.

It was a subject that had been broached on a few previous occasions, but Don had such horrible memories about his first book that he had always insisted he would never do another.

The author had simply sent him a tape recorder and blank tapes and told him to talk until the tapes were full. The editing was so heavy handed that it changed the sense of what Don was trying to say and he had no input into the peripheral areas such as format and pricing.

I told him that I would guarantee that this time, writing
a book would be easy for him. I didn't go so far as to suggest
he would enjoy it, but I assured him that he wouldn't hate it.
To win him over, I appealed to his responsibility to hockey.
I told him that he should look upon it as his legacy to the
game.

I pointed out that Americans can call upon a vast body of
work from football coaches, basketball coaches and baseball
coaches. But where would Canadians look to find the insights
into their game as provided by the great hockey coaches?

Scott Bowman refuses to write a book, and when
someone wrote a biography of him a few years ago, he not
only refused to cooperate, he asked everyone he knew not to
cooperate. Toe Blake never wrote a book. Nor did any of the
other leaders in playoff wins over the years: Al Arbour, Mike
Keenan, Pat Quinn, Glen Sather or Dick Irvin Sr.

I told Don that many Canadians pay close attention to
his opinions and regard them highly. As an example, I told
him about a recent chance encounter I'd had in St. Andrews,
the tiny town in New Brunswick where I live. I stopped to
chat with a lady who had a small boy with her. "Is he skating
yet?" I asked.

"Oh, no," she answered. "Don Cherry says kids shouldn't
skate until they're four, and he's only three."

A couple of years before that Heathrow meeting, I had
suggested to Don that we should do a book entitled *The
Code*, which would explain Don Cherry's rules for playing
hockey the way it should be played. The publishing company
Random House even made a prospective cover for it, and it
looked fantastic.

At that stage of his life, however, Don still wasn't in the

mood to do a book. But after the Heathrow meeting, he changed his mind. Perhaps Tim talked him into it. Perhaps I did. He never said.

Whatever it was, a couple of weeks later he called to say that he would do the book, but he wanted to do it his own way. Instead of a structured exposition of hockey's code, he would simply string together his reminiscences and from that, the code would emerge.

He wanted to know if that would be acceptable.

It was certainly acceptable as far as I was concerned, but it wasn't my decision. I had promised Don that I would get him a good deal with a good publisher so I met with the Random House people, who had published one of my earlier books, *Go to the Net*, and told them what Don wanted to do. I also made it perfectly clear that if they agreed to do this book, their relationship with the author would be like none they had ever had before.

In essence, the conditions boiled down to the fact that Don would have to be treated with kid gloves. He hated his first experience with writing so much that I had promised him this project would not be the least bit onerous.

I met with all the people who would be involved, including the top executives at the publishing house, and they readily agreed to the terms.

To get the procedure rolling, Don and I met in a restaurant of a hotel that was fairly accessible for both of us (when you live in Toronto, this is how you think).

We talked for a couple of hours with a tape recorder on the table, and in the days to come, I put together some of Don's anecdotes—transcribed into standard English.

He didn't like what he saw.

His objection was simple. It didn't sound like Don. He wanted the book to come across as if the reader were in a pub listening to him tell stories.

So after that, we stuck to telling Don's stories in Don's own words and there were no more problems.

• • •

Don had a few more conditions, but for the most part they arose from his concern for potential readers. He had never forgotten his blue-collar days and he wanted to make sure that as many fans as possible could afford to buy the book. Therefore, he insisted that the selling price had to be less than $30.

He also said that the book had to be substantial. He didn't want to turn out a slim, large-print effort that wouldn't give readers their money's worth.

He wanted to provide the photographs so that readers got an insight into his life, not just a bunch of wire-service photos.

If the Random House people had any qualms about accepting all Don's conditions, we never saw any evidence of it. They quickly agreed to anything he suggested.

Rather than having us meet in hotel restaurants, Don bought three tape recorders—one for the living room, one for the bedroom and one for the den where he watched games until the wee hours. Whenever he thought of an anecdote, he recorded it. He would bring the tapes to the CBC studio on Saturday night and hand them over in an envelope when no one else was around. He wanted the two jobs—author and analyst—to be kept separate.

For the most part, my job was easy. I just transcribed the

stories—enjoying them in the process—collated them and
checked a few facts.

The result was *Don Cherry's Hockey Stories and Stuff*, one
of the bestselling non-fiction Canadian books in history.

•   •   •

Brett Hull never hid his feelings about teammates who didn't
live up to expectations. For that matter, he never hid his
feelings about anything.

He had no qualms about shaking his head in disgust if a
teammate made a poor pass during a game, and in practice,
his observations were often scathing. At one morning skate,
when Hull was paying no attention, as usual, the coach
announced that they were to reverse their sticks for an
upcoming drill. When Brett didn't do it, a teammate told
him of the order.

"As if it makes any difference to you which end of the
stick you play with," said Hull.

•   •   •

Brian Sutter was one of the many coaches with whom Hull
didn't see eye to eye.

One night, during Hull's tenure with the St. Louis Blues,
the team took a bench penalty.

"Go and serve it," Sutter said to Hull.

"I don't serve bench penalties," said Hull, staying firmly
rooted on the bench.

"Go and serve it," said Sutter with a little more vehemence.

"No way," said Hull. "I don't serve bench penalties."

Sutter was a tough guy and by now, he was angry. "Get
over there!" he shouted.

Hull, never known as one of hockey's great pugilists, figured discretion was the better part of valour and skated across the ice.

A few seconds before the penalty ended, Sutter sent one of the other players over to deliver a message. Hull was to stay on the ice and rush into the play when the penalty expired.

Once the Blues had killed the penalty, Hull emerged from the box and, like a grandfather out for a Sunday skate on the local pond, casually headed for the bench.

"Stay on," shouted Sutter, waving his arms frantically. "Stay on."

Hull kept coming to the bench and climbed over the boards as a replacement dashed to join the play.

"I told you to stay on!" shouted Sutter.

"And I told *you* I don't serve bench minors," retorted Hull.

•   •   •

One night when the Blues were in Los Angeles, the game was tied in the last minute and Hull was on the ice.

The faceoff was to be in the Kings' end, and out came one of the St. Louis checkers to replace Hull. Sutter wanted to protect the tie and get the game into overtime, and Hull was never known as a great defensive player.

Hull didn't move. "Brian sent me out," said the other player. "You're supposed to go off."

"I'm not going," said Hull. "Get off yourself."

From the bench, Sutter was screaming at Hull to get off the ice. Hull shook his head and stood his ground.

Finally, the intended replacement left so that the faceoff could take place.

From the faceoff, the puck came back to Hull, who rifled it into the upper corner to put the Blues in front.

He came off the ice shaking his head. "Like we're going to play overtime in Los Angeles," he snorted.

• • •

When Brett was playing for Team USA in the Nagano Olympics, he was often seen devouring Japanese culture. In other words, he frequented the same bars as many of the media.

But Brett devoured a bit more of the culture than we did. In the literal sense. We figured that by sampling sushi, miso soup and the like, we had been sufficiently reckless.

Hull, however, had no qualms about downing a helping of one of the snacks the Japanese like to enjoy with their beer—roasted crickets.

Hull said that they actually tasted all right, and he offered a little hint just in case we wanted to try a roasted cricket ourselves (we didn't).

"You have to make sure you put it in your mouth sideways and not longways," he explained. "If you don't, when you bite it, the legs spread out and it feels kind of funny."

• • •

There are many reasons why Scott Bowman was the best coach in NHL history.

One of them is that he understood how to get the most out of his superstars.

In February 2010, when he was asked about Washington Capitals coach Bruce Boudreau's handling of Alexander Ovechkin, Bowman said, "When you've got a star like

Ovechkin, you've got to make sure you're in his corner 100 per cent of the time. And he is."

This is the way Bowman handled his stars from Glenn Hall in St. Louis, to Guy Lafleur in Montreal, all the way through to Steve Yzerman in Detroit: Bowman would go to the star players and ask them about their preferences. Which linemates did they want? How did they want to travel? What defencemen did they want on the ice with them? Which hotels did they want to stay at?

Whatever the star wanted, he got. In Mario Lemieux's case—during Bowman's tenure with the Pittsburgh Penguins—he didn't even have to practise. He felt it detracted from his game performance. So, while his teammates practised, Lemieux relaxed.

But once Bowman had made all these concessions, the star had no excuse for anything less than excellent play.

Should his performance falter, Bowman could go to him and say, "You're supposed to be a great player. Why aren't you showing it? You're given everything you want."

It was a highly effective approach.

Just because a player has plenty of talent doesn't mean that he's going to be dominant.

On the 1992–93 New York Rangers, Mark Messier and coach Roger Neilson were constantly at odds. Neilson was a student of the game and he insisted that it be played his way. Messier had his own ideas and they didn't mesh with Neilson's, especially with regard to the manner in which the power play should be run. The Rangers, despite enjoying the highest payroll in the league, missed the playoffs.

The next season, Mike Keenan took over as coach. As one of Bowman's disciples, he knew what to do. He gave

Messier free rein and let him use whatever strategy he liked with the power play.

With essentially the same team that Neilson had left him, Keenan won the Stanley Cup.

● ● ●

Jean Beliveau may be the classiest man I ever met. It sounds odd, but there is something about his presence that makes you respect him, even before he says a word. And when he does talk, he does it with both an elegance and eloquence that precludes any sort of interruption or argument.

Veteran hockey writer Red Fisher tells a story that demonstrates what kind of person Beliveau is:

The mother of one of Red's friends spotted Beliveau in a store near her house. Not being a sports fan, she couldn't place him, but she knew that her son had a picture of him and that he must therefore be important.

She approached Beliveau and asked him for his autograph. He, of course, complied.

While he was signing, the woman asked, "You're a football player, aren't you?"

"Yes, I am, madam," said Beliveau.

Typically, Beliveau was far too gracious to risk hurting the woman's feelings by correcting her. Her son had no difficulty recognizing whose autograph she had acquired. When she went home and showed it to him, Beliveau's name was clear. Many athletes scribble something illegible when asked for an autograph. Not Beliveau. "If people care enough to ask for an autograph," he explains, "it is my responsibility to give them one they can read."

● ● ●

Marian has a favourite Beliveau story of her own, one that illustrates that he was just as classy at the height of his fame as he was in later years.

She was in high school in Berkeley, Michigan, a suburb of Detroit, in 1963, when there were only six teams in the NHL. For some reason, she was a Canadiens fan and wrote to Beliveau asking for an autographed picture.

In her letter, she explained that all her classmates were Detroit fans and they gave her a hard time whenever the Red Wings beat the Canadiens.

Beliveau not only sent the requested coloured photograph (most were black-and-white in those days) and autographed it, he also added a personal note on the back.

"Thank you for your nice letter and kind words," he wrote. "I hope that we win all our games in Detroit so you have life a little easier."

•   •   •

Brett Hull may have had his selfish moments, but he took the game as seriously as anyone else in the league—perhaps more seriously.

When he was with the Dallas Stars, he infuriated coach Ken Hitchcock one morning by flipping the puck into the corner during a two-on-one drill (where two forwards go to the attack against one defenceman).

The first time he did it, Hitchcock ignored him. But when he did it again, Hitchcock charged at him. "What are you doing?" he screamed.

"Dumping it in the corner," snapped Hull. "That's all you ever want to do. I'm just doing what you want."

Hull got sent off the ice for that one, but he did it

because he cares about the game and he firmly believed that Hitchcock's style did not capitalize on the team's abilities.

In Game 3 of the 1999 Stanley Cup finals, Hull got crunched in open ice by Buffalo's Alexei Zhitnik, a notorious low hitter. He staggered to the bench and found a spot beside Joe Nieuwendyk.

It was not a random selection. Throughout his career, Nieuwendyk had been plagued by a series of knee injuries.

"Joe, what does it feel like when you've wrecked your knee?" asked Hull.

"It either hurts a lot or it's numb," said Nieuwendyk.

"It's numb," said Hull.

"Then you're done," said Nieuwendyk.

"Oh, no, I'm not," said Hull. "I've got to play."

He missed the rest of that game and he missed the next one as well. There was good reason for that. He had a torn medial collateral ligament.

But in Game 6, it was Hull, parked on the edge of the crease at 14:51 of the third overtime period, who fired home the goal that gave the Stars the Stanley Cup.

• • •

There's a lot of travel in hockey and there appears to be even more on the way as the NHL continues to give the impression that it may expand even further.

No matter what Gary Bettman says for public consumption, the governors feel that a 32-team league would be far superior to the present 30-team league, if for no other reason than simple arithmetic. It would allow for two 16-team conferences with eight teams making the playoffs and eight missing, an aesthetically superior concept to eight in and seven out.

When I started covering hockey in 1973, most of the teams were in the eastern part of the continent, and road trips were therefore short. Once or twice a year we'd swing through the far west—to Los Angeles, Oakland and Vancouver—but other than that, we weren't away much. Then, during the seventies, the league expanded into other markets and absorbed four teams from the World Hockey Association (WHA). By 1980, there were franchises across western Canada—in Vancouver, Edmonton, Calgary and Winnipeg.

For varying amounts of time, Denver, Atlanta and Kansas City were also represented. Now, there are franchises in Anaheim, Miami, Dallas, Tampa Bay, Raleigh-Durham, Denver (again), Phoenix, Nashville and San Jose. In 1997, Atlanta was awarded its second NHL franchise, the first having moved to Calgary in 1980. Both St. Paul and Columbus had their expansion bids accepted at the same time.

Travel is a breeze for teams located in the eastern seaboard of the United States—even though it's much more extensive than it used to be—but if you cover a team in the Western Conference, you can rack up a six-figure frequent-flyer balance in a real hurry.

The rewards on those programs are considerable, and in the pre-Internet days when sportswriters travelled freely, they were only half joking when they said that their motto was "Points 'R Us." Many of them took European vacations in the summer, or at least travelled extensively in North America, and the frequent-flyer programs were often the source of the tickets.

Even today, many of them still rack up good mileage and when they get to Europe in the summer, they're never surprised to run into a referee or linesman. If you've ever got a question about maximizing your points, those are the guys to ask.

● ● ●

At one time, when teams had a lot of commercial flights, the frequent-flyer miles were an area of negotiation. Not every team wanted the players to have the points. As a result, some players got their agent to guarantee the points through a clause in their contract.

Now, teams fly charter all the time, so it's no longer a concern.

Travelling in comfort on a charter flight, players can relax, wander around the plane and even take their pants off if they want to. This last might not seem to be a particularly important consideration to most travellers but it can be a boon to an athlete who needs to apply ice to a leg injury or get an aching muscle massaged.

Most players love charter flights, although not all of them are clear on the concept. There was, for instance, Brent Thompson, a former player for the Winnipeg Jets and Los Angeles Kings, who earned the nickname "Two People" in part because he boarded a charter flight and asked the attendant if he could have an aisle seat. The incredulous flight attendant first thought it was a joke, then, when she realized it wasn't, tried to stifle a grin as she said, "You can sit anywhere you want, sir; it's a charter."

His ever-compassionate Kings teammates called him "Two People" after that, explaining to him that they had decided no one person could be that stupid.

● ● ●

In an earlier era, it was never wise to fall asleep on a flight. As often as not, a player who made that mistake would wake up with a pile of shaving cream on his head. If the airline crew cooperated, there would be a maraschino cherry on top.

Because travel can be such drudgery, the players did whatever they could to alleviate it, and that often translated into practical jokes. The Canadiens' Yvon Lambert once took his boots off during a flight and fell asleep. He was well into the terminal, padding along in his stocking feet, before he got his boots back.

In Boston's Logan Airport, for instance, there was a store that sold live lobsters. Over the years, many ill-fated crustaceans found their way onto a hockey flight. Hockey humour being what it is, there was invariably great mirth and merriment when an unsuspecting player reached into his carry-on bag in midflight and a disgruntled lobster latched onto his fingers.

Weighing down a teammate's suitcase was also a hockey-humour staple. When the Vancouver Canucks played in the Pacific Coliseum, they'd often practise there, then leave immediately for a road trip. As a result, many of the weights from the training room made more than one circuit of the continent. Someone would slip a weight into a teammate's bag while he was in the shower, but at the first opportunity, that player would transfer it to someone else's luggage.

One of the dumbest travelling practical jokes in history was perpetrated by Serge Savard in his first year as a player with the Montreal Canadiens. A fashionable prank at the time was to set fire to the bottom of a newspaper while a teammate was reading it, then shout, "Hot news!" It wasn't a particularly clever move in a hotel lobby or restaurant, but when Savard did it on an airplane, it was downright dangerous. Coach Toe Blake told him that if he ever did such an idiotic thing again, he would have played his last game with the Canadiens.

• • •

Savard, of course, went on to an illustrious career as a player and general manager, and over that period, the calibre of his practical jokes improved considerably.

His best may have been the one he pulled shortly after one of Canada's brightest hockey moments, the victory over the Soviet Union in the memorable 1972 Summit Series.

Savard's old buddy and former teammate John Ferguson had served as an assistant coach on the Canadian team, and throughout the eight-game series, Ferguson had managed to get the entire Russian team to sign a stick.

This was no mean feat. The Soviets were extremely regimented and reclusive at that time, and this was their first exposure to the Western world. They were heavily supervised and not supposed to have any interaction with the Canadians. The KGB contingent attached to the team made sure of that.

Furthermore, none of them spoke English, so it was not surprising that it took Fergy the full eight games to acquire all their signatures. In fact, it was surprising that he got them at all.

Naturally, Ferguson treasured his memento. As the Canadian team checked in for their flight back home from Moscow, Savard assured Ferguson that his stick would be safe if it were put in with the luggage.

Ferguson snorted in derision and said there wasn't a chance that he would even remotely consider such a prospect.

Clutching the stick to his chest, he boarded the flight then sat with it between his legs. Savard, of course, insisted that it would be safe in the overhead luggage compartment. Ferguson wouldn't hear of it and even took the stick with him to the toilet, knowing full well that if he left it in Savard's care for even a few seconds, something untoward would happen.

Finally, the plane touched down in Ottawa where a full-scale state reception was planned for the national heroes. Military bands serenaded their arrival, and the receiving line was headed by the prime minister, Pierre Elliott Trudeau.

The coaches went first, then the assistant coaches, then the captains. Ferguson was an assistant coach and Savard was a captain, so they were standing close to each other.

As the line progressed, Ferguson, still clutching his stick, was told by the prime minister that the country was proud of its hockey heroes.

"And we never forgot our duty as Canadians," chirped Savard. "That's why Fergy here brought this stick back as a gift for you."

"Well, thanks very much," said Trudeau, taking the treasured stick out of a speechless John Ferguson's hands.

• • •

It was one of the greatest practical jokes in hockey history and Savard was delighted to have been its perpetrator, even though he knew that, the relationship between himself and Ferguson being what it was, there was bound to be some retribution.

However, from Ferguson's point of view, the story had a happy ending.

The prank was such a classic that Savard couldn't help but brag. As a result, the Montreal media got to hear of the joke, and it made such an entertaining story that a couple of us wrote about it.

There was no Internet in those days, but the Prime Minister's Office (PMO) in Ottawa got daily copies of all the major newspapers.

When Trudeau saw the story, he returned the stick to a grateful Ferguson.

SIX

Life lessons from Bowman

When Scott Bowman was coach of the Montreal Canadiens, he had to deal with five newspapers, each one trying to outdo the other. In English, there were the *Gazette* and the *Montreal Star*; in French, *La Presse*, *Le Journal de Montreal* and *Montréal Matin*.

Every off-day morning when the team was in town, we'd troop down to the Forum for the morning skate, head into Scott Bowman's office and get his pronouncements for the day. Often, he'd comment about his own team or one of his players. Once he'd finished, we'd head into the dressing room for confirmation, denial or amplification.

It was no accident that if you were to look back at the Montreal newspapers of those days, you'd find that the prime hockey story was the same in all five papers.

Some days, Bowman would comment about the Canadiens' upcoming opponent. That might require a follow-up phone call, but usually, Bowman would provide enough information that we could get by on his quotes alone.

When he left Montreal, he went to the Buffalo Sabres until 1987 when he was fired. (By then, he was general manager. He's very proud of the fact that he was never fired as a coach.)

Without a real hockey job, he joined *Hockey Night in Canada*.

When that happened, our relationship changed. We were now colleagues, and one day in Calgary, we went for lunch together.

We chatted about a number of things, and at one point I said, "You know, Scott, you were always great to deal with when you were a coach. You made our life easy. Every day, you'd give us something to write about."

Bowman looked at me as if I was missing out on something—which I was. "Well, you don't want the media thinking for themselves," he explained. "You let them think for themselves, there's no telling what they might write."

•   •   •

To my mind, Bowman understood the media game perfectly and as a result, he was always one of my favourite people to deal with—and not just because he catered to my inherent laziness.

Not everyone shares my sentiment. There's no doubt he is calculating in his dealings with the media, which turns some people off.

Others say they don't like him because he lied to them. I always found that to be nothing more than an admission that they didn't really understand their own business. Of course he lied to them. Name a GM or coach who hasn't lied to the media. When asked about a player's injury, a potential trade, an off-ice incident or any other aspect that they feel might somehow result in damage to their team, GMs and coaches invariably lie. If a writer were to break off relationships with every hockey man who lied to him, he'd soon be living a solitary life.

When I worked in Montreal, I got more exclusive stories than my colleagues for one simple reason: Bowman gave them to me.

But it had nothing to do with me. Anybody working for the *Gazette* would have been given the same stories.

When Bowman wanted to shake up the team—which was often—he'd make some inflammatory comments. Not all the players could read French, though all could read English, so for his comments to be effective, they had to be in an English paper. The *Star* was an afternoon paper, so the players couldn't read it before practice. Hence, by a process of elimination, Bowman had to use the *Gazette*. I was eternally grateful.

•   •   •

It was Bowman's theory, passed along to him by Toe Blake, that players should never be allowed to get complacent. (It's no accident that Bowman's disciple, Mike Keenan, always adhered to the same theory.)

Even though Bowman coached a great team in Montreal in the 1970s—probably the best in hockey history in relation to the other teams of its era— he never let the players bask in their glory.

One afternoon in Minnesota, he decided that Steve Shutt would be a healthy scratch. There was no justification for it. Shutt was the left-winger on a line with Guy Lafleur and Pete Mahovlich, arguably the most feared line in the game at the time.

The players were in an uproar. A delegation was dispatched to Bowman's suite to complain. Shutt's benching was rescinded. The Canadiens won 6–0.

That's how things went.

One morning in Washington—a very early morning—we were waiting for our commercial flight to board, and I was nursing a major hangover and still half asleep when Bowman walked over and began a conversation in typical fashion.

"Cournoyer, eh?"

"Cournoyer? What about him?"

"Not effective anymore, eh? Trying too many things. Just like Lambert."

"What's the matter with Lambert?"

"What's *right* with him?"

And so it went, with Bowman rhyming off half a dozen players whose game was in need of serious revision.

I couldn't take out my notebook because that would have attracted the attention of the other reporters. So when I got back to Montreal a few hours later, I wrote the story from memory.

Needless to say, the quotes would not have been exactly as they came out of Bowman's mouth, but that's the way we did things in those days. As long as the content was valid, no one complained about the wording.

I had no problem identifying Yvon Lambert and Yvan Cournoyer as a couple of Bowman's targets. Then I added the others to the story as I remembered them. The problem was that I remembered Larry Robinson as coming in for criticism.

The next day, Bowman called me aside.

"I didn't say anything about Larry. There's nothing wrong with his play."

"Oh. Sorry about that," I said.

"It doesn't matter," said Bowman. "Don't worry about it. It won't do any harm to shake him up like the rest of them."

• • •

During the 1998 playoffs, I was bouncing around from one series to another, depending on the interest that was being generated at the time.

At one point, when the St. Louis Blues were in the midst of their series with the Red Wings, I was sitting in Bowman's office getting his views for a story. In typical Bowman fashion, he interrupted one of his answers to change the subject completely.

"Gretzky's hurt, eh?" he said.

"He is? What's wrong with him?"

Since Gretzky was playing for the Blues at the time and the team was denying any injury, this information seemed to be worth following up.

Bowman replied he didn't know what was wrong, but said it was clear from the way Gretzky was skating that he was not physically sound.

I wrote the story and headed to the airport to move on to another series. When Bowman's quotes became public in the next day's *Toronto Sun*, he was approached for a comment by the writers covering his series and denied he'd ever said such a thing.

The newspaper business being what it is, many of the other papers took great delight in running a story saying we'd been wrong.

I'd known Bowman far too long to point out in print that I had his quotes on tape, and let it slide for a few days, until I returned to the Wings' series. I ran into him in one of the concourses under the stands and said, "You know I've got that quote about Gretzky on tape."

"Yeah, yeah," he said. "I gotta go."

And off he went.

The next day, he called me into his office. "Close the door," he said.

Then he tossed over a confidential internal NHL document that subsequently made a very good story. "I just happened to see this lying around," he said. "I thought you might be intcrested."

That's why I say Bowman understood the media game perfectly. Both sides have responsibilities. If you screw up, you make amends, and life goes on.

● ● ●

Every hockey fan is familiar with Wayne Gretzky's skills as a player. But unless you played with him, you probably don't know of his proficiency as a video camera.

"If you ever stop and talk to him, he'll recall every play," said Glen Sather, who was Gretzky's general manager and occasional coach during his days with the Edmonton Oilers.

In that era, the videotaping of games was not universal, as it is today, and as a result, there was often no visual evidence of a play. That didn't matter to the Oilers. They just called on Gretzky to find out what had happened.

"He could tell me not only where everybody on our team was on the ice at any time," recalled Sather, "he could tell you where everybody on the other team was on the ice."

● ● ●

In the NHL, there are two kinds of penalty shots. In the first instance, a player who is hauled down takes the shot.

But on rare occasions—such as when an opponent closes

his hand on the puck in the crease—a penalty shot is awarded to a team, and the coach gets to designate a shooter.

Anyone who was on the ice at the time of the infraction is eligible.

Naturally enough, players clamour for such an opportunity. When one arose for the Ottawa Senators in 2006, coach Bryan Murray was considering his options, when the players started piping up and suggesting Chris Phillips.

Phillips is a defenceman and not a particularly prolific scorer, so unless he's Marc Crawford at the Olympics, a coach won't usually consider selecting a defenceman over a forward.

But Phillips had been with the Senators for his entire career, so Murray, who was in his first year with the team, decided to listen to the players. "I thought he must be really good at it or something," he explained.

He wasn't. Phillips floated a feeble shot into the pads of Carolina Hurricanes goaltender Cam Ward.

It turns out that Phillips had been given some advice by his teammates. "They told me to shoot right at his pads," he laughed. The theory was that he'd miss and might perhaps pick a corner, but as it happened, he was right on target.

So why did the Ottawa players pick Phillips? He hadn't had a goal in the entire season and his teammates wanted him to crack the slump. And they had a 5–1 lead at the time.

• • •

Mario Lemieux and Wayne Gretzky were the dominant players of their era.

But Lemieux's contributions to the game are a pale shadow of Gretzky's. Gretzky always put the game first. Lemieux always put himself first.

This is not a criticism of Lemieux's talent. When he wanted to be, he was brilliant. That fact is indisputable. He won two Stanley Cups, an Olympic gold medal, a World Cup championship and a host of individual trophies. But only for brief stretches was he the dominant player in the game.

He started badly, refusing to go to the podium when he was drafted by the Pittsburgh Penguins in 1984. On the advice of his agent, Gus Badali, who was also Gretzky's agent at one point, he opted to remain in his seat, a move that could only be interpreted as an exhibition of disdain for the league that he was about to enter.

Then for four years, he wandered in the wilderness, unable to lead the Penguins to a playoff spot.

It was not until the 1987 Canada Cup, when he teamed up with Gretzky and scored the winning goal in the memorable three-game championship series against the Soviet Union, that he finally learned what it took to be a winner.

On the opening day of that series, Gretzky went onto the ice and stood shoulder to shoulder with head coach Mike Keenan. At Keenan's other shoulder stood Mark Messier. It was an expression of support for the coach from two dominant players. Lemieux stood on the fringe of the cluster of players who were gathered around.

During that tournament, Gretzky and Messier began the hockey education of Lemieux. They included him in their off-ice activities and they passed along the trade secrets of winners.

Two seasons later, Lemieux made the playoffs. Two seasons after that, he led his Penguins to the first of their back-to-back Stanley Cups. At that point, he seemed poised to become the greatest player in NHL history. But it was not to be.

He was plagued with back problems, rarely practised with the team and created the widely held perception that he didn't really care about the game.

He did what needed to be done but little more. He was guarded in his dealings with the media. He turned down more invitations to play for Canada than he accepted. He complained loudly and often about the state of the NHL, at one point comparing it to "a garage league."

He missed the 1994–95 season because he contracted Hodgkin's disease, and although he battled it successfully and returned to the game, he retired two years later at the age of thirty-two. For the next three years, he was all but invisible. He ignored hockey, and if he was seen in public, it was invariably at a golf tournament.

When the Penguins filed for Chapter 11 bankruptcy in 2000, it was revealed that the team owed him US$26.2 million. His only realistic chance of getting that money was to assume a share of team ownership. So that's what he did. And he came out of retirement.

Once again, there were flashes of brilliance. At one point in the 2002 Olympics, a Swedish broadcaster said he was "skating like an old tractor." But in the gold-medal game, which Canada won, Lemieux was superb.

Over the next two seasons, he played only thirty-six games before he retired again.

And true to form, when his Penguins advanced to the Stanley Cup final in 2008, he steadfastly turned down every interview request, even though he attended every game.

There can be no doubt that Gretzky loves hockey. If Lemieux does, he keeps his passion well hidden.

•   •   •

When the Hull brothers played hockey for the Chicago Blackhawks from 1965 to 1972, Bobby was by far the better player. But Dennis was—and still is—a lot funnier.

After his hockey career ended, Dennis found his true calling as an after-dinner speaker, and today he's a top draw at sports-related banquets. He is truly hilarious and most of his stories are told at Bobby's expense. I always liked one better than the others.

"Everybody remembers Bobby as a great scorer," says Dennis, "but they don't think of him as a tough player. But he was. In fact, in one season alone, he put three people in hospital."

At this point, Dennis pauses for a moment. Then he adds, "Of course, they were all in the maternity ward."

• • •

Gary Roberts had a great career as an NHL power forward and he openly gives a lot of credit for his success to his two linemates in Calgary, Joe Nieuwendyk and Sergei Makarov.

Roberts and Nieuwendyk grew up together in Whitby, Ontario, and broke into the NHL together. The Flames' primary enforcer at that time was Tim Hunter, and in his first year, Roberts played as if he wanted to emulate Hunter.

Nieuwendyk didn't think that was a good idea. "When we first broke in with Calgary," Nieuwendyk said, "there was me, Gary and Timmy Hunter. Gary was fighting all the heavyweights, then we sat around in the summer and I said, 'Man, you're not going to make a lot of money fighting your whole career. You had better learn how to score some goals.'"

When Sergei Makarov was given his release by the Soviet

Ice Hockey Federation and joined the Flames, that concept turned into a reality.

"When we played with Makarov," said Nieuwendyk, "Gary's job was simple: Go to the net. I think Gary led the league in two-foot goals."

Roberts did so well with Makarov and Nieuwendyk as linemates that he started to close in on every forward's dream—a 50-goal season.

"Makarov was incredible," said Roberts. "Makarov set me up for all those empty nets. When I was at forty-nine, I told him, if I get fifty, I'll name my first son Sergei."

He got the 50. But did he fulfill the promise?

"No," said Roberts. "I had a girl, thank God. And we never had any others."

•   •   •

In the New York area, a certain radio reporter I'd better not identify never misses a chance to show up at any event that might provide a free meal. He helps himself to any piece of memorabilia that can be subsequently sold online, and generally makes a nuisance of himself.

When Al Arbour was coach of the New York Islanders, the media crush wasn't what it is today, and rather than stage a full-scale press conference after the morning skate, Arbour would simply hold forth in his small office.

But when the Islanders advanced in the playoffs one year, the office became a bit crowded and the reporter in question found himself at the back of a group of media people with no way to get his microphone near Arbour.

There was, however, a toilet cubicle adjacent to Arbour's desk, so the reporter went in, climbed on the toilet seat, leaned over the partition and stretched towards Arbour with his microphone.

Frank Orr, the hockey writer for the *Toronto Star*, looked at this performance and said in his usual laconic drawling fashion to everyone within hearing range, "If you hear a splash, flush it quickly."

• • •

When you're in the media business, memorabilia comes and goes.

You're often given various items that commemorate an event such as a Super Bowl, a World Series or a Stanley Cup final, and you occasionally get items offered to you by players.

I never bothered with any of those things until my first son was born in 1978, then I started acquiring some stuff with the idea that he might want it some day—which he did.

These items aren't necessarily valuable. I have, for instance, a couple of the plastic rats that became an integral part of every goal celebration by the Florida Panthers during their run to the 1997 Stanley Cup final.

I have a large champagne-cork collection, having picked up a cork from the floor of every Stanley Cup–winning team's dressing room for more than twenty consecutive years. But since I'm the only one who can attest to their provenance, the corks have no real value.

I used to have some valuable hockey sticks, including the last one Wayne Gretzky ever used as an Edmonton Oiler, but they were stolen from my basement in Toronto.

A few young lawyers lived upstairs and the house had a communal basement which was used primarily for storage.

During an out-of-control party thrown by the lawyers, people were wandering around in the basement and the sticks disappeared.

And I once had an Yvan Cournoyer sweater that predated my career as a hockey writer. In fact, it was of 1960s vintage when sweaters had laces at the neck.

When I started covering the Canadiens, we stayed at the old Statler Hilton hotel in Buffalo, indisputably the most decrepit hotel on the circuit. Its only redeeming factor was that it was adjacent to Sinatra's Bar, a great watering hole owned by the Sinatra family. No, not *that* Sinatra family.

Two brothers ran the place—one was called Frank (really, I am not making this up)—and they were hockey fans. They thought it might be a good idea to put some memorabilia on display, so on one trip I brought along my Cournoyer sweater, which had by now been autographed by its previous owner. The Sinatras were going to borrow it for a year. Wally Harris, one of the top referees at the time, agreed to provide one of his sweaters as well, and for a while—much more than a year, as it happened—they were up on the wall in Sinatra's Bar.

But for one reason or another, I missed a couple of scheduled trips to Buffalo and when I finally got back, the bar had suffered the same fate as the Statler Hilton. As part of a renovation project, it had been demolished.

I never saw my Cournoyer sweater again.

• • •

Keith Jones was one of those players who, as a result of a series of injuries, never lived up to his potential. Instead, he retired early and became a hockey analyst on television where his sense of humour stands him in good stead.

One day, during a radio interview, he explained that as a result of his media duties, he watched every game he possibly could.

"That's my life," he said. "I do nothing else. All I ever do is lay on the couch every night and watch hockey on television."

"That's all?" asked the interviewer. "You're a married man. What happens if your wife decides that she wants to get amorous?"

"Okay," conceded Jones. "Once in a while, I miss a shift."

•   •   •

"Satellite Hot Stove" was the brainchild of John Shannon, who was the executive producer of *Hockey Night in Canada* at the time.

Every week, Shannon would read the Sunday newspapers and see notes columns by the country's hockey columnists. Invariably, those columns would be full of rumours, gossip and insights that had not been a part of a six-hour television production Shannon had supervised a few hours earlier.

The original "Hot Stove" had become a part of *Hockey Night in Canada* broadcasts in 1939, and it too had featured hockey gossip. But despite appearing to be unscripted, it was, in fact, well planned, even to the point of having "ad-libs" created by a staff writer in midweek.

In fairness, it must be pointed out that Canada was at war at the time, and according to the government's censorship laws, every word spoken on the CBC was supposed to be scripted.

(As an aside, I should perhaps explain the origins of the name of the segment. I do this because I have been asked by

young people over the years why it has a stupid name like
"Hot Stove." In Canada's earlier days, before central heating
became standard in most houses, a pot-bellied wood-burning
stove provided warmth. These stoves sat in the middle of
kitchens and stores all over the country. Many towns had no
electricity, and this was an era long before television, so in
winter, people would sit around the "hot stove" to indulge in
the primary form of entertainment—conversation.)

The original "Hot Stove" segment lasted more than thirty
years before it was replaced by gimmicks like Peter Puck and
Showdown, but in 1995, Shannon resurrected it, and it lives
on to this day, albeit in a less provocative fashion.

•   •   •

In its first couple of years under Shannon, the "Hot Stove"
panel fluctuated slightly, but it gradually evolved into a
standard trio—John Davidson, Jim Hughson and me.

In general, Davidson provided the league's point of view;
I provided the players' point of view and Hughson provided
his own point of view.

Because players tend to be more talkative and less guarded
than team owners and league executives, I often brought
up items that were more speculative than those offered by
the other two. In many cases, they were rumours and we
identified them as such.

Critics liked to say that many of these rumours came to
nothing and had no substance. That was half right. Of course
they often came to nothing. For every trade that is made, ten
are discussed. We might say in all accuracy that a trade was
being negotiated, but for one reason or another, the trade
was never consummated.

But the critics were wrong when they said that the stories had no substance. We never, under any circumstance, made up a story. There was never any need to do so. So many stories of interest were floating around in the players' world that there was never any need to fabricate them.

The problem was that in many NHL cities, there is a cozy relationship between the media and the team. Stories that might be construed as embarrassing are swept under the rug. On the "Hot Stove," we tried to get all the gossip out there, and as a result, Shannon spent many a Monday morning trying to calm down an irate general manager.

In most cases, he succeeded, but not always.

On one occasion, when Eric Lacroix was playing for the Colorado Avalanche and his father, Pierre, was the general manager, the team was struggling. In an attempt to hammer out some problems, one of those infamous players-only meetings was held. But one of the players told me that Eric was so mistrusted by his teammates that he was excluded from the meeting.

When I mentioned that on "Hot Stove," Pierre Lacroix went wild. He said I had made his wife cry and that it was outrageous that I should embarrass his family in this fashion. The fact that the story was totally accurate didn't appear to concern him in the least.

Lacroix never talked to me again. Even though on a number of occasions we were side by side—even alone in an elevator on a couple of occasions—he acted as if I were a piece of furniture. It didn't matter much. He was never a good source anyway.

• • •

Hockey Night in Canada has never run as smoothly as it did when John Shannon was there. He cut through the prevailing union-made mentality and demanded accountability from some of the CBC staffers who rarely encountered such an approach.

We were to tape one Saturday afternoon at 3 p.m., and at 3:03, as the soundman was busy hooking up my microphone, Shannon came storming into the studio.

I'll chop the expletives, but his rant went something like this: "Let's get one thing straight. The satellite window opens at three o'clock and this show starts at three o'clock. That means that he [pointing at me] is wired up and ready to go. It means that all the lighting is ready. It means that the cameras are ready and everything is in place. Is everybody clear on that?"

There was no answer. There didn't need to be.

Shannon never said a word to Lianne Harrower, who has done the *Hockey Night* makeup for years. He just gave a quick look in her direction that said, "I know you do your job, Lianne, but while I'm here, I might as well warn you I don't want any slippage on your part."

Lianne and I both remember that Shannon tirade well. It was typical of him. He was always demanding and he could occasionally explode, but if you did your job properly, you never had anything to fear from him.

SEVEN

Trouble in paradise

My problems at *Hockey Night in Canada* began when Shannon got fired and was no longer there to protect me. Shannon had guts and always ran the show in a professional fashion. He wanted maximum disclosure and if we stepped on a few toes, so be it.

When he left, the show was run by bureaucrats who wanted a warm, worry-free life that did not include fielding angry phone calls on Monday morning. Eventually, I became one of the many people who were sent packing by Nancy Lee. Considering the others she had dumped before me, I figured I was in pretty good company.

Lee started at the CBC in 1987 as a sports reporter. By 1994, she had become head of radio sports, a department that at that time was one of the most highly acclaimed of its type in the world. Within two years, it had become a shell of its former self. As a result, her position was no longer demanding.

Lee eventually was moved up to become deputy head of TV sports.

Because of this rise in status, she was somehow identified as someone to watch within the corporate hierarchy. By 2000, she had been named executive director of CBC Sports.

In interviews, she repeatedly made it clear she was concerned with promoting women in sports.

"Now that we've established ourselves as executives, the big challenge now is getting women on TV where they'll be seen," she told the *Toronto Star*. "The sad thing is that [women in sports] is still a story. It's my job to make sure that in ten, fifteen, twenty years' time that it's still not as much of a story."

Within seven months, she had fired Shannon, even though he was widely regarded as the best TV hockey producer in the world and earlier that year had been named by the *Hockey News* as one of the ten most powerful people in the sport. Shannon went on to establish *Leafs TV*, subsequently became the National Hockey League's senior vice-president of broadcasting and is now a hockey analyst on SportsNet.

In the next few years, Lee also fired or forced out a number of other talented CBC staffers, including announcers Chris Cuthbert, now with TSN, and Brian Williams, now with CTV.

Williams is so well respected that he was the anchor on CTV's coverage of the 2010 Olympics. Cuthbert, who won a Gemini Award for his calling of the 1998 Grey Cup game, is the top-ranked hockey announcer on TSN and did the play-by-play of the most-watched show in Canadian television history, the 2010 Olympic gold medal game between Canada and the United States.

Lee created a position that was ironically labelled—considering how many CBC Sports properties were lost during her regime—manager of program acquisitions for CBC television sports and hired her friend Sue Prestedge to fill it. Then she fired Cuthbert citing budgetary restrictions.

Lee also dumped Paul Graham, another excellent producer, who moved on to handle the televised games of the Toronto Raptors of the National Basketball Association (NBA).

In the summer of 2004, Lee told Don Cherry that she had no intention of renewing his contract when it expired at the end of the following season, even though she had failed badly once before when she tried to use a similar tactic on another high-profile member of the *Hockey Night in Canada* lineup.

The intended victim that time had been Ron MacLean, but she had badly underestimated Ron's popularity, and when the news of his release broke, there was a monumental national outcry with front-page stories in all the major papers. The subsequent backlash forced the CBC to consider public opinion for once and send the matter higher up into the nebulous hierarchy that determines the corporation's policy.

Lee was overruled and Ron signed a new contract.

During Lee's tenure, the CBC lost such valued and traditional properties as Toronto Blue Jays baseball, the Toronto Indy, the Vancouver Indy, the Grey Cup, CFL football and the Brier. In addition, even though the CBC had always carried the Olympic Games, Lee was unable to secure the rights to the 2012 Olympics in London, England, and even the 2010 Winter Olympics, which were held right at home in British Columbia!

With the dealine for renewal of the *Hockey Night in Canada* contract coming precariously close, Lee left in October 2006.

●　　●　　●

In his days as a player, Murray Wilson, who went on to be a part of the Montreal Canadiens broadcast team until he retired after the 2009–10 season, was, arguably, the fastest skater in the league. His teammate Yvan Cournoyer was no slouch either, but by the time Wilson joined the Canadiens, Cournoyer was slowing down a bit.

The problem was that in those days, the training regimen was much more of a hit-and-miss affair than it is now, and Wilson seemed to spend more time nursing sprains and pulled muscles than taking part in the games. Furthermore, he seemed to be injury prone. He even missed a few weeks once because he slipped on a piece of popcorn in the dressing room.

On one occasion, after recuperating from one of his injuries, Wilson remained relegated to the press box. Wilson was well liked by his teammates, and before long there were anonymous player complaints in the newspapers that he should be playing, not watching.

Accordingly, at a game-day morning skate, coach Scott Bowman called the team together. "I understand you all think that Murray Wilson should be back in the lineup," he said.

Murmurs of assent were heard from the assembled players.

"Fine," said Bowman, "then he'll be back in the lineup tonight."

More murmurs of assent.

"So which one of you wants to sit so I can put Wilson in?" asked Bowman.

Now there was nothing but silence.

"Thought so," said Bowman before resuming practice.

• • •

Once upon a time, there used to be lots of trades in the National Hockey League.

Unfortunately, however, Gary Bettman's salary cap, which requires every serious fan to be more familiar with accounting procedures than hockey attributes, put an end to the trading mentality.

There are very few trades these days, and those that are consummated are not trades of players as much as trades of contracts.

Because of the salary-cap limitations, no team wants to take on a big salary unless it can unload a big salary. But if you've got a $5-million hockey player who isn't performing, how are you going to get another team to agree to take him off your hands? There's only one way. You take back another player who isn't performing—or maybe two—but the salary-cap hit will be identical.

No one thought, for instance, that the Toronto Maple Leafs would ever get out from under Jason Blake's onerous contract. As it happened, though, the Leafs were able to trade Blake, along with Vesa Toskala, to the Anaheim Ducks for Jean-Sebastien Giguere.

But to get rid of their obligation of approximately $8.25 million to Blake and $1 million to Toskala, the Leafs had to take on an obligation of approximately $9 million to Giguere.

The salary cap was sold to the fans by Bettman as a means of saving the small-market teams and creating a level playing field.

It was no such thing. It was a way for owners to create a degree of cost certainty and increase their profits. The fans didn't enter into it.

•   •   •

Before the salary cap, when trades were still commonplace, they were sometimes blockbusters that became part of hockey lore. The ten-player deal that sent Doug Gilmour to the Toronto Maple Leafs from the Calgary Flames, for example, is still talked about today. But mostly, the trades, though frequent, were just routine—a team needing a defenceman trading away an excess forward, for instance.

It's probably more than coincidence that since the imposition of the salary cap, the security of general managers has become more precarious. In the pre-cap era, a GM could usually outlast four or five coaches before he himself got the axe. The reason for this was that he could easily give the appearance that he was helping the team improve. He could make deals, and then blame the coach if the new players didn't do any better than their predecessors.

To cloud the issue a little, he could also toss in the ubiquitous concept of "future considerations," which used to appear so frequently in NHL trades. Since these were usually kept secret, it was difficult for the fans to criticize a trade. Because the salary cap is so pervasive, future considerations are now rare.

But the truth of the matter is that often, there were no future considerations. They were just a smokescreen, but it took someone like Bob Clarke to admit it.

When he was GM of the Philadelphia Flyers, he traded defenceman Sergei Klimentiev to the Nashville Predators for future considerations.

Since Klimentiev had been an all-star in the American Hockey League (AHL), the Philly media corps pressed Clarke for an explanation of the future considerations.

"Really, there are none," admitted Clarke. "We traded him for a tenth-round pick in a nine-round draft."

• • •

Fans always think that a lot of science goes into hockey trades. In some cases, there is indeed a great deal of research and evaluation.

But sometimes, they are based on nothing more than a whim.

There was, for instance, the time when the Chicago Blackhawks were going through one of their many slumps and the coach of the era, Bob Pulford, decided that the blame could be laid on the fact that too many of his players had their minds on matters other than hockey, namely females.

Accordingly, he delivered a sermon concerning the attendant evils thereof and warned that there would be serious consequences for the next player who appeared to be putting women ahead of hockey.

Defenceman Dave Feamster was sharing an apartment with Doug Crossman at the time and driving a Corvette. He was also receiving occasional visits from a lovely lady who happened to be a Playboy bunny. When she decided to go shopping the morning after Pulford's speech, it was agreed that the trio would drive to Chicago Stadium, then she could use the car for a couple of hours while the guys were practising.

With the Corvette being a two-seater, the girl sat on Crossman's lap and, as fate would have it, they rolled into the Chicago Stadium parking lot at the same time as Pulford. The coach took one look at Crossman and the girl and blew a gasket. Before the morning was over, the innocent Crossman had been traded to Philadelphia.

• • •

I always hated covering the Olympics. They're a tremendous spectacle to watch, but working them is another story altogether.

The security is ramped up and mostly enforced by volunteers who feel the need to justify their presence by being officious.

"You can't go through that gate."

"But I want to get to that spot right there on the other side."

"Yes, but you can't go through that gate. You have to walk half a mile down to the other gate, then walk back."

"Why can't I go through that gate?"

"That's the rule."

As for getting the story, access is the only thing that really matters. Everybody in the world can watch the same Olympic event as you on television. If you have no more access than the viewer, what's the point of being there?

After every NHL game, you're free to go into the dressing room and talk to the players. At the Olympics, you have to stand in what, for reasons that are typically Olympian, is called a mixed zone. Since there is no mixing at all, only the curious form of logic displayed by an Olympic bureaucrat would call it that.

The media stand behind solid barriers and the players parade past on their way to the dressing room. They may or may not stop. If one stops and you're talking to him, others you might want to talk to can walk past. Once they're gone, they don't come back.

If you do get a player to stop, an Olympic volunteer puts a stopwatch on the interview then tells the player to move along.

"It's okay," the player might say. "I don't mind."

"No, we have rules. You have to move on."

There's also the problem that once a player stops, a number of people who were somewhere else in the mixed zone decide that they want to hear his answers, so they charge up, crushing you against the barrier as they try to get their microphones within range of the player.

And because of the sheer magnitude of the Games, travel to and from the venues is appalling, even when the buses are on time, which is not often the case. There's also the language problem. You often have to work through an interpreter.

And worst of all? Hardly anyone reads what you produce. The Olympics are a TV spectacle—a great TV spectacle. People love to watch them, but they don't really want to read about them a day later. Newspaper editors have never understood that point.

• • •

After Canada won the hockey gold medal at the 2002 Olympics in Salt Lake City, there were no more competitions, so the Canadian media decided they would all go for dinner. Bruce Garrioch, of the *Ottawa Sun*, and I had been hanging out a lot during the Games and he suggested we go along.

"Not a chance," I said. "I've been to too many of them. They all know that the bill gets split equally at the end. Guys whose dinner will be one appetizer if they have to pay for it themselves will have four courses. Stephen Brunt will whisper to the waiter that he wants something like a nineteenth-century cognac that costs a fortune—as he invariably does. I've subsidized those guys too often. Let's just go to the pub we've been going to for two weeks."

Garrioch agreed. In Salt Lake City, with the drinking laws being restrictive, there weren't a lot of good places. But we'd found one that had decent food, brewed its own beer and had a great ambience.

During the course of our dinner, every Canadian player came into that place. Some stopped to chat briefly. Others stayed for a while. Theoren Fleury sat for more than an hour, his gold medal around his neck and a non-alcoholic drink in front of him.

Theo was an old friend, and at that time, he had just come back to the NHL after a stint in a rehab facility. Having won the gold, he was on top of the world. The smile never left his face the entire time he was there.

It had been a tough battle back for him. He had hit rock bottom and contemplated suicide, but he was always a likeable guy and a lot of people had done their best to help him.

We talked about that and I asked him who he was proudest of.

"Me," he said.

•   •   •

I was the hockey columnist at the *Globe and Mail* in 1988, and, as such, was expected to go to Calgary for the Winter Olympics.

"No way," I said. "I hate covering Olympics. I'll stay and cover the NHL."

Most of the players on the Canadian hockey team were amateurs, and throughout the Games, the NHL schedule continued uninterrupted.

The powers-that-be persisted. I had to go. I also persisted: I wasn't going.

I rarely went into the office, but one day, I got a call from the secretary, Joan Astley, asking me to come in to fill out my request for Olympic accreditation.

"Today's the last day," she said. "You have to come in and do it."

"Perfect," I said. "I'm not coming in, so by tomorrow, it will be too late and this whole thing will be settled."

If anyone were to check that accreditation request for the 1988 Olympics, they might notice that my signature was forged. A very talented lady was Ms. Astley.

•   •   •

I had held out for so long that it had boiled down to a battle over principle. The *Globe and Mail* didn't like to have their staff deciding what they would or would not cover and finally insisted that I had to go.

Or else.

But long before I finally acceded, extensive coverage plans had been made, and even though I was the hockey columnist, James Christie had been assigned to cover Pool A hockey—the pool that contains the top-seeded teams. It seems they hadn't been convinced that I would give in.

James is a fine writer, so the coverage wouldn't suffer.

I was assigned to the B Pool. I had no problem with that. Basically, it boiled down to a nice two-week Calgary vacation at the *Globe*'s expense. The B Pool had teams like France and Austria. Sweden was the only Scandinavian hockey power of note in those days, so Finland and Norway were in the B Pool as well.

My workday was about thirty minutes long and, after a long evening, I'd often be trooping into our residence as some of the more conscientious staffers were getting up to go off and cover their events.

I'd stagger out of bed around noon and do a piece for CBC Radio. Since everyone else was off covering the Games, I was the only one they could get.

I'd have a leisurely lunch (or breakfast, if you want to get technical), then around 4 p.m. head over for the press conference with the two coaches of that day's B Pool game.

I'd bang out seven or eight quick paragraphs, then head off for the media hospitality lounge to check out options for the evening. By virtue of my slack workday, the responsibilities of entertainment coordinator had fallen upon my shoulders

Terry Jones, of Edmonton, no stranger to evening entertainment himself, was there along with a few others. "How was the B Pool?" someone chortled.

"Fine," I said. "I've churned out my six inches of copy."

"That's big-time stuff," said Jones. "Those grudge matches between Poland and Norway."

"Norway?" I said.

"Yeah. That's the game you allegedly covered. Poland and Norway."

Not long afterwards, the *Globe*'s sports desk in Toronto received a call.

"You know that B Pool story I sent a little while ago? Wherever it says Finland in there, change it to Norway, okay?"

•   •   •

In Montreal, hockey writers often stay at the Sheraton Centre Hotel on Boulevard René-Lévesque between Stanley and Drummond Streets.

The reason is the usual one that affects writers' decisions—

frequent-stay points—but there's also the attraction of the proximity of hockey history. For me, it's impossible to walk along either Drummond or Stanley into that hotel without being aware that I'm walking past the birthplace of hockey as we know it.

It's a building that now houses a rental-car outlet, but in the nineteenth century, it was the Victoria Skating Rink.

Because the property was rectangular, the ice surface took on the same shape. Prior to that, most ice rinks had been oval, but because the first indoor hockey game was played there in 1875, hockey in North America is now played on a surface that is 200 feet (61 m) by 85 feet (26 m).

The first Stanley Cup playoff was staged there in 1894, and it still gives me a chill to walk past it.

• • •

Because Igor Larionov had endured the hockey system of the Soviet Union, he was familiar with dictatorial regimes. However, he had expected a more liberal approach in the National Hockey League.

For the most part, that's what he got, but near the end of his career, he had the misfortune to find himself in the NHL's answer to the gulag—the New Jersey Devils organization.

Larionov signed with the Devils in 2003, thinking that as a veteran he could handle the edicts of GM/president Lou Lamoriello. The camera in the hallway to see whom players were talking to outside the dressing room he could handle. He accepted the lurking staffer who eavesdropped on every media conversation.

He even went along with the mandatory pre-game team dinners whenever the team was on a road trip.

But Larionov believed that mature NHL players should be allowed to make their own dining decisions. On most teams they are. As a result, as was his custom when having dinner, he decided to order a glass of wine.

He was told this was not allowed. Lamoriello's rules stipulate that no alcoholic beverages are to be consumed at the mandatory team dinners.

"I'm forty-two years old and I'm not allowed to have a glass of wine with dinner," fumed Larionov.

Such is life when you play for the Devils.

• • •

Larionov's term in New Jersey was not a good one. Not only did the ambience leave a lot to be desired, he missed almost half the season with injuries.

During that time, he was not allowed to interact with the rest of the team. Under Lamoriello's rules, injured players were to stay away from their teammates until they were ready to play.

However, they had to follow the team's rehabilitation schedule, and since they had to complete their workouts and be long gone before the other players showed up at the training facility, that meant they had to skate early—around 6 a.m.

Larionov dutifully showed up on time, donned his gear and went out to skate by himself. Almost immediately, he was called over by a team attendant and told to put his helmet on.

"I'm just skating," said Larionov. "I don't need a helmet."

"Lou's rules," he was told. "Every player must wear a helmet at all times when he's on the ice."

Larionov is one of the greatest players in hockey history. He has since been inducted into the Hall of Fame. But in the New Jersey organization, players are so disdained that they can't be trusted to stand up on skates.

After one season in New Jersey, Larionov retired.

• • •

By the 1970s, NHL teams no longer travelled by train. Some of the short hauls down the eastern seaboard were done by bus, but mostly the league used air travel—commercial air travel.

Montreal Canadiens general manager Sam Pollock was one of the pioneers when it came to using charters, which all the teams use now.

He contracted with a small local charter company to provide an old propeller-driven plane that was painted a hideous orange. Because of that and the fact that it looked like a bus with wings, Pierre Bouchard dubbed it the flying school bus.

But a hockey team travels with much more baggage than normal passengers, and as a result, the storage areas were inadequate. The only solution was to pile many of the team's equipment bags on the back seats.

Even in the coldest weather, we all had to stand around on the tarmac while the trainers crammed mountains of equipment bags onto the back seats. Then we boarded.

One night, however, a difficulty arose. All the extra weight on the seats caused the plane's tail to settle down onto the tarmac.

This was deemed to be a safety hazard. After all, the plane had just been refuelled, and a spark caused by its tail hitting the tarmac could, theoretically, cause an explosion.

Coach Scott Bowman soon found the answer. Before the equipment was loaded, the media had to board and sit at the front of the plane. This provided a counterbalance for the weight of the equipment at the back, and the tail stayed where it was supposed to be.

As far as Bowman was concerned, he had devised the perfect solution. If anything went wrong, only the media would be blown up.

• • •

Scott Bowman was never particularly popular with his players.

He worked them hard in practices and he was a strict taskmaster off the ice. On the psychological front, he worked hard to make sure the players never established a comfort level for themselves. As a result, the Montreal dressing room was rarely a happy place.

But the players put up with it for one very good reason, as Steve Shutt explained one day.

"We hate him three hundred sixty-four days a year," he said of Bowman. "On the three hundred and sixty-fifth day, we get our Stanley Cup cheques."

• • •

Bowman was only twenty-four when he took the Montreal Junior Canadiens to the Memorial Cup final. From there, he went to the Peterborough Petes as coach and general manager. Two years later, the Petes won the Memorial Cup.

Even though it was hard to get noticed in the days of the six-team NHL, performances like that gave Bowman a crack at an NHL job, which he took.

But there were no assistant coaches in the NHL at that time, and no one was likely to shunt Toe Blake aside and take over as coach of the Canadiens. As a result, Bowman had to settle for a scouting job.

Again, the prospects were limited. The junior teams were not independent franchises as they are today; they were owned by the various NHL teams. Furthermore, European involvement was non-existent. A scouting job therefore translated into watching minor hockey.

Bowman did this for three years and was getting increasingly restless. But suddenly, for Bowman and others like him, doors opened. In 1967, the NHL expanded overnight from six teams to twelve.

Bowman was given the opportunity to become an assistant general manager with the St. Louis Blues, and he jumped at it. Around that time, NHL teams were also starting to experiment with assistant coaches and since Bowman was already on staff, he got that job as well.

The coach and GM, Lynn Patrick, was an old-time hockey man and he was happy to delegate many of his coaching responsibilities. Accordingly, on the first day of their existence, the St. Louis Blues were exposed to Scott Bowman.

There were about fifty players in camp, and before the first practice got under way, Bowman called them over. "Let's get one thing straight," he said. "None of you deserve to be in the NHL. You all belong in the minors. The ones who stay in the NHL will be the ones who work the hardest. Let's go."

After sixteen games, the team had amassed an unenviable record of 4-10-2, and Patrick elevated Bowman to head coach. Despite having to overcome that poor start, Bowman took the Blues to the Stanley Cup final. He did it again the year after. And the year after that.

In the fourth year, he turned the coaching duties over to Al Arbour and the Blues lost in the semifinal. That's when Bowman left for Montreal.

As for his opening-day message to the Blues, Bowman says those who remember hearing it as stated above might be exaggerating slightly. But he admits to making it clear that if you were going to be part of his team, you were going to do it his way.

"I always took the philosophy that Toe Blake had," he explained. "A coach has to be a pretty bitter loser."

EIGHT
Asia sends a star to the NHL

In 1993, the Toronto Maple Leafs played a couple of pre-season games in London, England, an ideal ruse for a vacation disguised as work.

Accordingly, Scott Morrison and I decided to spend a week in London, at our own expense, with the excuse for the timing being that the Leafs were also in town. Morrison was at the *Toronto Sun* at the time and I was at the *Globe and Mail*.

We called upon the good relationship we had with the papers' travel agents and got ourselves an excellent deal to stay at the Royal Britannia Hotel, just behind Buckingham Palace.

A typical day went like this: I would get up and go for the "full English breakfast" (a nice little perk that was included in the room rate) then go and bang on Morrison's door.

Fifteen minutes later, roughly around ten-thirty, we'd meet in the lobby and head for the Burger King at nearby Victoria Station. He'd grab a breakfast croissant and a large coffee; I'd get a large coffee and we'd set off for our daily exploration.

I'd spent a lot of time in London, so I knew my way around, and it was not at all difficult to find an intriguing area to visit every day. We'd either walk to it directly or take the tube to a suitable stop, then walk around for the rest of the day.

This, however, didn't involve as much walking as it might seem. Because of the coffee we'd imbibed, we needed to relieve ourselves before long, and the best way to do that was to stop at one of London's many pubs. They open at 11 a.m.

Well, you can't just treat a pub like a public toilet, can you? So in addition to using the facilities, we'd have a pint each and head on our way. But before long, that pint had taken effect, so we'd have to stop at another pub. And so it went. At the end of the day, as if we needed it, we'd visit the hotel bar for a nightcap. London pubs closed at 11 p.m. in those days, but the hotel's hospitality was always available to registered guests.

The hotel bar was rarely busy, and one night we were standing at the bar chatting, when the only other patron, who had been sitting at a table by himself for a while, came up and offered to buy us a drink.

Not being unfamiliar with people who approach strangers in bars, we opted for the thanks-but-no-thanks approach. He asked us to change our minds, explaining that he frequently travelled to Canada and when he did so was invariably treated royally. Having overheard our conversation, he knew that we were Canadians and he wanted to repay the favour.

As this sounded reasonable, we changed our minds and had a drink with him.

More than one, actually.

It transpired that he was a Highland Scot whose first language was Gaelic. He now lived in Edinburgh and worked in the office of the Procurator Fiscal. That would be similar to the office of the Attorney General on this side of the ocean. He was a lawyer, but nobody's perfect, and the evening progressed pleasantly. Being a Scot, he was proud of his country's contribution to potent potables of the world and offered to buy us each a single malt.

Morrison was drinking rye-and-Coke and I was still on beer. We said we weren't really Scotch drinkers.

That, he said, was because we weren't sufficiently familiar with the golden nectar. Accordingly, he had the barman pour shots of ten different single malts. He then went through them one by one, explaining their intricacies. He added just a drop or two of water to each—it brings out the flavour, he explained—and we sampled them one by one.

Considering the prices in the Royal Britannia, he must have amassed a monstrous bar bill by the end of the evening. But he insisted on paying the whole thing.

Perhaps it's not true what they say about Scots and lawyers.

Or maybe he was lying about being a lawyer.

•   •   •

Naturally enough, the conversation turned to our reasons for being in London. We told him ours and he revealed that he was there to compare notes with the various investigative teams who were working on the Lockerbie bombing.

It had happened more than five years earlier—December 21, 1988, to be precise. A terrorist bomb had exploded inside Pan Am flight 103 when it was over Lockerbie, Scotland. All 259 people on board had died, and 11 Lockerbie residents had been killed by falling debris.

On that evening in London, we were given all sorts of inside information that had not yet been released to the public. We were told how the bomb had got on board, where it had been located and why it didn't explode on the first leg of the plane's flight from the Middle East to England.

"Do you think you'll ever find out who did it?" I asked.

"We know who did it," he said.

We were told that night—accurately, as it turned out—that two Libyans were believed to have been responsible. It was not for another seven years that they were brought to trial. With twelve years having passed since the explosion, the evidence was not as strong as it might ordinarily have been, and one was found not guilty. The other, Abdelbaset Ali Mohmed al-Magrahi was sentenced to life in prison. In Scotland, life in prison apparently means much the same as it does in Canada, so he was released in 2009.

But in view of the strained relations between Libya and the United Kingdom at the time of our discussion, it seemed possible that the bombers would escape prosecution.

"What happens if Libya won't cooperate?" we asked.

"That's why we have the SAS," said our friend.

The SAS is the Special Air Service. It's an elite arm of the British military and is widely conceded to be the best fighting force in the world.

• • •

One of the stories that still sends a chill up my spine was in one of my earlier books, *Go to the Net*.

When the book went on sale in 2005, I did one of those book tours that publishers like to organize—sending you from city to city to do five or six radio and TV interviews a day. Granted, not all the interviewers you meet have read the book, but in this case, most had, and it therefore seemed likely they'd want to focus on a story that until that time had never been published.

As it turned out, though, only one interviewer brought up the subject, even though it told of an event that could have changed the face of hockey as we know it.

It occurred on a hot summer night in 1981 when two superstars—one on his way down and the other on his way up—were almost killed.

The reigning superstar was Guy Lafleur. His successor was Wayne Gretzky. The two were in Montreal, attending training camp for Canada Cup 1981. One evening, as is customary in such circles, a bunch of the players got together for a few beers. That happened to be the one short period in Gretzky's life when he had a fast car, a Ferrari, to be precise, and he had brought it to Montreal from Brantford for the training camp. He had also taken it to the bar that night, but he didn't want to drive it back to the suburban hotel after drinking.

Lafleur agreed that Gretzky's decision made good sense. He himself hadn't had much to drink, he said. He would drive them back.

At that point, Gretzky wasn't even old enough to drink legally in the United States. He was still a kid—a kid very much in awe of Lafleur. As far as he was concerned, if Guy Lafleur pronounced himself capable of driving, there was no need for further debate on the subject.

On this particular occasion, Lafleur lost control and rolled the car.

One minute they were driving down the highway; the next they were upside down; then they were back on four wheels again. Neither was hurt.

God must be a hockey fan.

• • •

Gretzky told me that story many years ago, but he asked me to keep it quiet because it could make Lafleur look bad.

"If Guy ever admits it, you can use it," he said. "But if it's going to get out, I don't want it to come from me."

Lafleur finally broke his silence at the Heritage Classic in Edmonton in November 2003. That was the outdoor game between the Montreal Canadiens and Edmonton Oilers. Prior to the NHL game, there was a legends game involving some of the former stars of the two teams.

There was also a banquet honouring the old-time players, and some of them were invited to speak. When it was Lafleur's turn, he talked about the Montreal-Edmonton connection and told the story of flipping the car.

But English is Lafleur's second language and when he spoke of the car going over, he described it as "spinning." It spun all right. On its axis.

The story was out, but because of Lafleur's choice of verb, no one in the Edmonton media recognized its significance. Apparently, a lot of interviewers didn't either.

• • •

How long has it been since you saw a play called because the puck was frozen along the boards?

It used to be commonplace in hockey. Any defenceman who wanted to ease the pressure simply jammed his skate against the puck and held it against the boards. Within seconds, play was whistled down.

But nowadays, players poke at the puck and keep jabbing while one of the referees shouts, "Move it; move it." Eventually, the puck squirts out like a rugby ball coming out of a scrum, and play continues.

This is one of the legacies of John McCauley who was the NHL's director of officiating until his death in June 1989.

Both John's father and grandfather had died at the age of forty-three. When John reached forty-four, he made no secret of his relief. But he never saw his forty-fifth birthday.

McCauley had been a referee until he was punched in the face after officiating one of the games in the Challenge Cup in New York in 1979. Ironically, his assailant was not a hockey fan. He was just a belligerent customer at the restaurant in which McCauley and some associates were eating after the game.

No longer able to officiate because of permanent damage to his eye, McCauley took over the supervision of NHL officials and became both loved and respected by those who worked for him. One of those referees, Paul Stewart, even named his son McCauley.

And a favourite McCauley maxim that he loved to pass on to his referees lives on to this day: "A moving puck is a referee's best friend." That's why it's so difficult to get a whistle for freezing the puck against the boards.

• • •

One of the questions I am most frequently asked is: What is Don Cherry really like?

The answer is simple. Watch him on Saturday night and find out.

He may say things you don't like to hear, but they're what he believes.

He may say things that sound hard to accept, but when you check his record, which few of his critics bother to do, he has a remarkable accuracy rate.

He may blow his own horn somewhat, but even if he does, he's still in a minority in the media. Who else do you know who stands up for Don Cherry? If he doesn't do it, who else will?

With Don Cherry, what you see is what you get. When the camera lights go off, he lowers his voice a bit. But little else changes. This is not an act. This is Don Cherry.

He has a great reverence for the old-time values in life. He sticks up for friends. He hates bullies. He thinks our soldiers should be allowed to act like soldiers, not conciliators. He is patriotic. He believes in face-to-face confrontations, not sneak attacks. He believes that Canada produces the best hockey players in the world.

If you weren't already aware of all this, you haven't been paying attention to "Coach's Corner."

The only quality you may not have been aware of—although Ron MacLean mentions it on occasion—is Don's reverence for certain historical figures.

At one point, Don's three stars of history were: (3) Margaret Thatcher, (2) Sir Winston Churchill and (1) Lord Horatio Nelson. In recent years, however, T. E. Lawrence has displaced Baroness Thatcher.

But she's still highly regarded.

•   •   •

Don has no shortage of critics in the media. In fact, it's hard to find any Cherry supporters in the media.

In many cases, the simple reason for this is that most media people have left-wing leanings. Don certainly does not. And liberals, despite calling themselves that, are anything but.

It infuriates these people when Don suggests that a punch in the head is suitable retaliation for a cheap shot. To the media liberals, this is clearly a form of intolerance, and intolerance is never acceptable—unless it's intolerance of any views that are not left wing.

Don and I tend to share similar political views, so much so that when I was doing the "Hot Stove" at *Hockey Night in Canada*, I was not allowed to talk to him before his show. It was felt that whenever I talked to him, the subject quickly turned to political issues, which invariably got Don riled. "You get him worked up," they said, so I had to avoid him until he had done his show.

We have been friends for more than thirty years, but that doesn't mean that there is never a rocky moment. One came in 2008.

I was making regular mid-week appearances on *The Score*, doing a segment called "Ten-Minute Misconduct." There were three of us on camera and we would debate five topics for two minutes each. One night, the subject of overexuberance by Alexander Ovechkin was on the list.

Don had urged Ovechkin to calm down, saying that he was acting like a soccer player, and suddenly, in this hockey-mad nation, the entire country had become embroiled in a furious dispute.

On the air, I said, "As you know, I'm a good friend of Don's as well, so I'm a bit clouded on that.

"I wouldn't say Don is wrong.

"The only thing I would say is that there is a younger generation that is growing up that is younger than Don and I—considerably.

"These young guys look at it a little bit differently. I don't just mean the players. I mean the kids that are watching the games. They want to see these things.

"I'm sure that when the junior players started going along after a goal and pumping everybody's hand on the bench Don was opposed to that and yet now everybody in the NHL does it. It just comes as a matter of course.

"I think you've got to realize that you're selling this game, and especially in the market that Ovie is in, the kids come out there.

"This is a young generation. This is the Internet generation that goes to Washington Capitals games and I think they like that sort of stuff.

"You can go too far. I don't like the soccer stuff either and I agree totally with Don on that."

Don was furious. He felt that I had publicly demeaned him by saying that he had probably been opposed to celebrations by the juniors. He pointed out—at a decibel level of astonishing proportions—that he got along well with junior players, that he loved the way the kids play and that he watched them five nights a week.

I tried to point out that I had agreed with him, but he was not to be mollified. The next week, I took a transcript of my comments to the CBC and left it with him. The part that said, "I agree with Don totally," was highlighted.

After that, he seemed to accept that I was not part of the left-wing horde. When I got fired the following season, he was one of the first to call and commiserate. And when he decided to do a sequel to *Don Cherry's Hockey Stories and Stuff*, he called me to work with him again.

• • •

When Alex Mogilny played for the Toronto Maple Leafs, we would often chat. Sometimes it was about hockey, sometimes it wasn't.

He was a dedicated fan of English Premiership soccer, and that was a favourite topic. He was also an avid golfer, and he said that the biggest thrill in his sporting life was playing golf with Michael Jordan.

With Mogilny, you never knew whether he was joking or not, but there's no doubt that being in a tournament with Jordan was a memorable event in his life.

He once told me that the reason that his one-time linemate, Pavel Bure, had so many knee injuries was that he tied his skates too tight. By doing so, Mogilny insisted, Bure left no leeway. When he got hit below the waist, the ankles couldn't move, so the knees took the brunt of the blow. And knees are not known for their lateral flexibility.

As usual, I didn't know whether he was pulling my leg or not. It seemed like a strange theory to me, but I bounced it off a couple of other NHL people. They thought it was quite possible that Mogilny was correct.

• • •

At one point in the 2003–04 season, it appeared that Mogilny might become the first Russian to amass 1000 points in the NHL.

But he suffered a hip injury that year and missed more than half the season. While Mogilny was out of action, Sergei Fedorov overtook him in the scoring race and eventually claimed the honour for himself.

"That's too bad, Alex," I said to him one day after his return to the lineup. "I would have liked to see you get that milestone. But you were born in Khabarovsk, weren't you?"

Mogilny confirmed that he was.

"Isn't that about eight time zones east of Moscow?" I asked.

"Yeah, something like that," said Mogilny. "Eight or nine."

"So Asia starts at the Ural Mountains, Alex. You're way past that. You're an Asian. You'll be the first Asian to get a thousand points."

"Oh my God, Al," said Mogilny. "Don't go writing that I'm an Asian. I don't want people to think that I'm from out there."

So we left it at that.

A few weeks later, Mogilny got his 1000th point, and the Toronto media, microphones held out in front like lances, descended on him after the game to ask him about his achievement.

"Well, I may not have been the first Russian to get a thousand points," volunteered Mogilny, "but I'm the first Asian."

• • •

I started work at the *Globe and Mail* on Labour Day, 1980.

Let's put it another way. I first showed up for work at the *Globe and Mail* on Labour Day, 1980.

"Oh. You're here," said sports editor Cec Jennings. It was somewhat disconcerting that he placed the emphasis on the second of those three words.

"Well, yes," I said. "That's what we agreed on, remember?"

"Guess so," said Jennings. "Well, make yourself comfortable."

"Do I have a desk?'

"A desk?"

"Yeah. You know. A desk. A place to work."

This seemed to strike Jennings as something of a novel concept. It didn't seem to me to be such a strange request. At that time, the paper had forty-four people on its sports staff and even the most superficial research produced the conclusion that the other forty-three all had desks.

I eventually learned that this was just Cec's manner. He was by far the most easygoing, unconcerned sports editor I ever had—and I've had a lot. Nothing would dislodge Cec from his relaxed, unruffled state. I often got the feeling that if he were cutting wood and chopped his hand off, he'd look at it and say, "Oh. I guess I'm down to one hand now."

He led me to the back of the room where a desk was piled with three years of back issues of the *Racing Form*.

"I don't suppose anybody needs these," said Cec, just before he pushed them all onto the floor. "You can have this desk."

"Okay," I said. "What do you want me to do today?"

"Do?"

"Yeah. You know. Write?"

"Oh," said Jennings. "You'd better take a week or so to get used to the place."

This was my kind of paper.

•   •   •

By Friday afternoon, after a week in which my total contribution to the cause had been one cutline for one picture, and that was only because the guy who asked me to do it didn't realize I was the new columnist, I wandered up to

Cec's office and suggested maybe I should cover something—
like the Saturday Toronto Argonauts game for instance.

"I guess you could if you want," said Cec.

On Saturday, I dutifully wandered down to the stadium,
headed to the press box and ran into Allen Abel.

Al was the other sports columnist, but he'd been out of
town and we hadn't met since I joined the *Globe*. I knew him,
of course. In fact, he was the reason I almost didn't take the
job. When Scott Young left the *Globe*, I was asked to replace
him as sports columnist and even though it was a dream job,
I was so in awe of Allen Abel's superb writing that I said I
didn't think I could do it. To have Abel's column on one page
and my column facing it would be too embarrassing.

"Don't worry about it," I was told. "We don't want you
to try to be like Al. We love what he does, but we want you
to be opinionated, outrageous and outspoken."

That didn't seem like much of a challenge. I took the job.

● ● ●

Al sat beside me at the Argos game and started to tell me
about the inner workings of the *Globe*'s sports department.
Apparently, no one cared whether you came in to the office
or not. And if you did come in, no one really cared whether
you did any work.

If the paper sent you on a road trip, you were expected
to write, but at each end of the trip was a travel day—which
counted as a day of work—even if you were only making a
one-hour flight to Montreal.

The department's budget was determined at the end of
the year, and by a remarkable coincidence, turned out to be
the same amount as what had been spent.

It was not advisable to stint. The example given was the guy in the paper's London bureau who spent something like $900—a considerable amount in 1980—on a television for the office. He sent in the expense account and was queried as to why he had spent $2.98 on an extension cord.

As Al told of the paper's laissez-faire attitude and recited example after example, the game was proceeding, and it was the third quarter before I finally said, "This is not good. I haven't been paying attention to this game at all, and I've got to write a column about it."

"Weren't you listening to what I said?" Al asked. "Don't bother to write, nobody will care."

I didn't. They didn't.

• • •

After a couple of years, the *Globe* changed radically. The paper was bought by the Thomson Newspapers chain and suddenly the free-spending days came to an end.

A flight to Montreal no longer constituted a travel day. The company travel agent, who had catered to our every need, was sent packing and we had to use a commercial firm like everybody else. We always dealt with the same people and they tried hard to help us, but it was never quite the same.

Travel had to be telescoped. In the past, it had not been unusual to be wandering through a place like O'Hare Airport in Chicago and meet another *Globe* sportswriter.

"Where are you going?"

"Los Angeles. What about you?"

"I'm going home. I've been in Los Angeles."

Under the new regime, when you went on the road, every

effort was made to find two or three events for you to cover, not just one.

We cut out our annual trips to the Cactus League, a decision based upon the not-unreasonable assumption that Toronto interest in teams like the San Francisco Giants, Milwaukee Brewers and Chicago Cubs was somewhat limited. The annual coverage of the NFL meetings was scrapped as well—a shame because my supply of *Globe*-subsidized beachwear for NFL meetings at the Maui Hyatt was running low.

The contingent of horse-racing writers, which had numbered about five or so, was cut back to two. Copy editors who moved to other newspapers were not replaced. The woman who came in once a month to balance her bank book, file her nails and promise to do a story next month also disappeared from the staff.

A new publisher was hired. The *Globe's* publisher over the years had traditionally been a hardened old veteran of Canadian newspapers. This one was fairly young. And Irish. And an accountant.

When he started talking about elimination of the sports section on the grounds that it was expensive and didn't fit the *Globe's* corporate image, I knew it was time to move on.

I left the *Globe* for the *Toronto Sun* in 1994. The *Globe's* sports staff—forty-four people when I started—was down to thirteen.

NINE

The Gospel according to Sam

Unfortunately, hockey lags behind the other sports when it comes to literature.

In the United States, there are hundreds of books by and about athletes and coaches, some active, some retired, in every sport Americans consider to be important. But in Canada, perhaps because our primary sport is hockey and hockey players tend to be unduly modest, we don't have that wealth of literature. I've been trying to talk Scott Bowman into doing a book for years, but he won't do it.

He and I once sat at a table with Cliff Fletcher, Bob Clarke, Pierre McGuire, Bob Gainey, superagent Don Baizley and a number of other hockey luminaries and discussed this subject. Also there was my friend Jim MacDonald, a representative of the average fan. At the time, he was the head of the English department at Humber College.

I made the point that it was Bowman's responsibility to the game and to the people who love hockey to produce a book.

His knowledge is so all-encompassing, I said, that it should be shared.

I wasn't trying to earn money from any such arrangement;

I just wanted Bowman to reveal some of his secrets for the good of the game.

Everyone at the table agreed with my stance. But Bowman feels, with some justification, that if he were to explain his success, it would be tantamount to bragging. Also, if he were to explain how he had outsmarted another coach, that coach would be embarrassed, and as a premier member of the close-knit hockey community, Bowman doesn't want to do that.

It seems reasonable to assume that hockey fans would love to read a book by Bowman, just as they would enjoy the insights of people like Cliff Fletcher, Bill Torrey, Lou Lamoriello, Ken Holland, Jacques Lemaire and many others.

But generally, hockey people are too unassuming to write them.

•   •   •

Former Canadiens general manager Sam Pollock could have written a magnificent work, but it goes without saying that he wouldn't have dreamt of doing so.

He could have explained his strategies for success and illuminated those strategies with some real-life examples.

I'm sure there were dozens of them. But from my own experience when I was covering the Canadiens, here are, in no particular order, the principles that I feel Sam would have enumerated if he had been forced to reveal his own Ten Commandments for running a hockey team.

1. Every game is important.

As far as Sam was concerned, it didn't matter whether it was a late-season game after you'd clinched first place—and there were many such games for the Canadiens in Sam's day—or a pre-season exhibition game. You always played hard and you always played to win. If you got away from that principle at any time, you might also get away from it at the wrong time.

2. The team that gets the best player wins the trade.

Sam was under some heat in Montreal when he traded away Billy Collins, Mickey Redmond and Guy Charron to get Frank Mahovlich in 1970. All three youngsters had great potential, whereas Mahovlich was thirty-two in an era when players rarely played past thirty-five.

But the Canadiens won the Stanley Cup in Mahovlich's first season, and they won it again two years later. Pollock readily conceded that in total talent, he had given up more than he had received. But he had acquired the best player in the deal and won two Cups in the process. Neither Collins nor Charron ever won the Cup. In fact, Charron played twelve years and never even made the playoffs. Redmond never won a Cup after the trade.

3. Take away as many excuses as possible.

This was a theory that Scott Bowman elevated to an art form when dealing with his star players. But all the players in Montreal were well treated. They travelled well. They were well paid, and they were treated fairly. They were expected to produce, and it was Sam's intention to minimize the number of reasons they could have for not doing so.

4. Always give a disgruntled player a second chance.

It was not unknown for a player to feel slighted, especially during Bowman's tenure as coach. When that happened, a player might storm up to Sam's office and ask to be traded. Invariably, he got a sympathetic ear and a promise that if he still felt the need to leave, it would be arranged. Then nothing would happen. But if a player demanded a trade for a second time, he could go home and start packing. He'd soon be moving.

5. *Stockpile goalies.*

Any serious hockey fan knows that the goalie is the most important player on the team, especially in the playoffs. So if you have a lot of goalies, it stands to reason that you have a better chance of finding one who can fill that all-important position. Goalies tend to develop later than other players, so a kid who hardly seems to be worth acquiring just might develop into a quality goalie.

6. *Never let the players get complacent.*

This too was evident in Bowman's coaching strategy. But Bowman was very much a disciple of two people—Toe Blake and Sam Pollock. Think of how many times you've seen a player be a healthy scratch, then rebound with a series of solid performances. It took a benching to shake him out of his complacency and prior to that point, he had produced a number of lacklustre games. Pollock felt that if you took away the complacency, you got strong performances more consistently without that string of lacklustre games leading up to a player becoming a healthy scratch.

7. *Have a no-tolerance policy for dressing-room rifts.*

Although no one in the Montreal organization would ever speak for the record about this, I was led to believe that Sam had a strict policy in the area of French-English relations. At a time when separatism was on the rise, this was an extremely volatile area in Montreal. Occasionally, when a sudden trade of a youngster came about, there were suggestions that the player had made an anti-French or anti-English remark. In this arena, there were no second chances. And it must be said that although French-English rifts on the Canadiens were often rumoured, I never saw any evidence of them. Stories alleging that such divisiveness existed were invariably written by people who had very little interaction with the team or who had a political axe to grind.

    8. *Be prepared to sacrifice players to hurt opponents.*

Sometimes, Sam would make deals that were not intended to have any direct or immediate effect on his own roster but would still pay dividends.

One such deal was his 1971 trade of Ralph Backstrom to the Los Angeles Kings for Gord Labossiere and Ray Fortin. To no one's surprise, neither ever played for the Canadiens. But Backstrom played very well for the Kings—so well that he prevented them from slipping into the basement. Instead, the California Seals stayed at the bottom, and Pollock just happened to own their first draft pick. He used it to select Guy Lafleur.

In 1973, the Boston Bruins were the biggest threat to the Canadiens' supremacy. In fact, it was widely believed that if the Bruins had a top-notch goalie, they could conceivably knock the Canadiens off their perch.

Fortunately for the Bruins, they had the sixth pick in the 1973 June draft, and a top-notch young goaltender by the name of John Davidson was about to graduate from the Calgary Centennials. No goalie had ever been selected as high as sixth, so even though the Bruins would be setting an NHL precedent, they would be getting the goalie they so badly needed.

The Canadiens had the fifth pick, but they also had Ken Dryden, so the Bruins felt safe. But Pollock was aware that the St. Louis Blues also needed a goalie. He gift-wrapped his pick and sent it to the Blues with the understanding that they would take Davidson.

The Stanley Cup finals were played in May in those days and as one Montreal staffer told me, "Sam feels it's just as important to screw the Bruins in June as it is to screw them in May."

9. Never trade draft picks unless you know what you're giving up.

That matter has been discussed elsewhere in this book. Simply put, if you're going to trade draft choices, you have to know what's involved. If you're giving away your pick once the season is over, that's fine. But if you do it before the season, when you have no idea where you're going to finish in the standings, you run the risk of disaster.

10. Establish a strict pay ladder.

Even before a salary cap was imposed and player salaries were made public, Pollock knew that the players would compare paycheques. The best player on the team got the most money. Second-best got the second-most and so on. An imbalance in the team's salary structure could easily evolve into dissension—and on some teams, it did.

Pollock was the one who made the evaluation and he stuck to it. In fact, he was so firm on the matter that he let Ken Dryden sit out an entire year rather than pay him more than Lafleur.

• • •

Wayne Gretzky's father, Walter, never missed a chance to collect a souvenir of his son's career.

When Wayne was playing in Edmonton, he would go through feast and famine like any other player. If the famine dragged on for too long, Oilers general manager Glen Sather always knew the cure. He'd place a call to Walter Gretzky.

"Whenever we needed a big win, or it was a big game, or if I was struggling, Glen would fly my dad in," recalled Gretzky. "He'd never tell me about it. I'd come out for the morning skate and look and my dad would be sitting there behind the bench.

"I'd turn to Slats and say: 'I guess I must not be playing that well, huh?'

"He'd say, 'Just a little something to get you going.' Nine out of ten times it would work. I think as a kid, you really enjoy seeing your parents in the stands. I don't think NHL players are any different whether they're nineteen or twenty-nine or thirty-eight; they love to look up and see their family there."

For his part, Walter Gretzky never wasted a trip. He'd always pick up a memento or two. Or three. The world's largest Gretzky museum is in the family home in Brantford, Ontario, and in those days, Walter also snapped photographs everywhere he went.

"He kept everything," said Wayne. "My dad was a pretty astute guy in that he covered the fundamentals no matter what it was in life. Even when I was young, he used to yell at me if something got lost. He collected everything with a passion.

"He never collected it to sell. My dad, if he was down to his last penny, wouldn't sell one thing of mine. He would give it to charities to raise money for charity, but he would never sell it for personal use."

• • •

Right from Wayne Gretzky's first days in professional hockey, his father was able to envision the larger picture. Most parents willingly agree to anything that the team might produce as their son's first hockey contract, but Walter offered advice. One of the things he urged Wayne to do was to make sure there was a clause in his contract that gave him possession of any game-worn material or game-used equipment. And Wayne Gretzky never disobeyed his father in hockey matters.

One day after his career had ended, Gretzky read an article in the paper discussing one of the money-making ventures of Oilers owner Peter Pocklington. He couldn't help but smile.

"I read where Peter Pocklington sold all the Oilers' old sweaters," he said with a laugh. "Whoever bought them didn't get *my* sweaters. Those sweaters that were sold were definitely not mine. They might have my number and name on them, but they weren't ones I wore, because I've got almost every sweater I wore.

"Glen [Sather] might have asked for the odd sweater and I gave it to him, but other than that, no one in the Oilers organization got my sweaters. I kept every one.

"They're either in my parents' house in Brantford or in my restaurant or in the Hall of Fame. I don't know whose sweaters the guy got, but they're not mine. I have them."

● ● ●

When Wayne Gretzky broke in with the Oilers at seventeen, the team was in the World Hockey Association (WHA), a league not known for fulfilling its responsibilities to its players in a first-class manner.

As a teenager, living away from home, travelling around the continent and not short of money, Gretzky could easily have fallen into the many traps that await young people in such circumstances.

He didn't, partly because his parents had instilled proper values in him and partly because Ace Bailey took him under his wing.

Bailey's real name was Garnet, but no one ever called him that. He was always "Ace," a reference to the player Irvine Wallace "Ace" Bailey, who Eddie Shore almost killed in 1933. Shore hit Bailey from behind and knocked him unconscious. He remained in critical condition for two weeks and although he eventually recovered, he never played again. It was in order to raise money for Ace Bailey that the NHL staged its first all-star game.

The modern-day Ace was similar to his nominal predecessor in that if you were going to hit him, you'd better do it from behind so he couldn't see you coming. He was a rough, tough, physical player who was never unwilling to fight but didn't do it very often because it was well known that he rarely lost.

He took care of Gretzky both on the ice and off it. One night, however, Sather had decided to keep Bailey on the bench, and an opposing player by the name of Bob Dillabough seized the opportunity to take advantage of the situation. Every chance he got, he rammed Gretzky. Wherever Gretzky went, Dillabough went with him to slash, elbow or crunch him.

Bailey watched all this from the bench. When Gretzky came off, Bailey said, "Next shift, bring the puck over here along the boards."

Gretzky did so and Dillabough followed. That was as far as he got. As soon as he came within range, Ace reached over and unloaded a haymaker onto his chin. Dillabough went down, out like a light, and Ace continued to sit, a look of total innocence on his face.

• • •

Bailey was Gretzky's roommate, and one day, they overslept their afternoon nap.

They still had time to make the pre-game warm-up, but only barely. They dashed to the car, rushed to the rink and ran into the dressing room. The other players were already starting to go on the ice.

"Never mind about me," said Bailey, helping Gretzky with his equipment. "If I miss the warm-up, no one will notice, but if you're not out there, it will be a big deal."

Thanks to Bailey's help, Gretzky got onto the ice shortly after the rest of the team, and sure enough, his brief absence went unnoticed.

Bailey then turned his attention to himself. He put on his underwear, stepped into the shower and turned on the jets. Then he went back and put on his skates and hockey pants. When the team came back in, there was Bailey, sitting soaked and looking exhausted.

"One of the toughest warm-ups I ever had," he announced. "Look at me. I'm drenched in sweat."

• • •

After his playing career ended, Bailey became a scout. He was not an alcoholic, but nor was it a shock to see him in a bar after a game. As a result, he knew the media guys, and was one of our favourites.

He had a zest for life and as someone once said, if a hockey player could ever be described as Runyonesque, it would be Ace.

By 2001, Ace had become the director of scouting for the Los Angeles Kings, and with training camp a few days away, he was leaving his Boston home to go to Los Angeles for team meetings.

Somehow, he miscalculated and his alarm went off an hour later than it should have. In a rush that was reminiscent of the time he and Gretzky overslept their nap, he raced off to Logan Airport, breaking a few speed limits along the way. He dashed in and made the plane with literally seconds to spare.

Also on the plane was one of his protegés, Mark Bavis, another Kings scout. It was United Airlines flight 175 to Los Angeles.

Less than an hour later, it crashed into the World Trade Center.

• • •

In the Montreal Forum, the best press-box seats were accorded to the local media. The *Gazette* had one at centre ice. Right next to it was the seat for someone from *La Presse*.

I knew most of the guys from the other papers, but every so often someone new showed up and on this occasion in 1974, it was a large guy in his early thirties. During a stoppage of play in the second period, he turned to me and said, "You Henglish?"

To the Québécois of that era, anyone whose first language wasn't French was considered to be English, so I said that I was.

"I 'ate all Henglish," he said.

"Really? How many have you met?"

"You da firs'."

That was my introduction to Réjean Tremblay. He had been hired by *La Presse* out of Chicoutimi, Quebec, and spoke no English, so the paper sent him on a Berlitz course for three days and pronounced him ready to cover the Canadiens.

At that time, he was something less than worldly. On one of his first road trips, he was complaining loudly at breakfast about the hotel in which we were staying. His alarm clock hadn't worked properly, and no matter what he did to the thermostat, he couldn't sleep because he was too hot.

It turned out that instead of setting the alarm for 9 a.m., he had in fact set the electric blanket on high.

• • •

In Chicoutimi, Réjean had been a high-school teacher— Latin and Greek—so we often talked about things other than hockey. Over the years, we became good friends, and at one point, he even bestowed upon me the status of *bleuet honoraire*— honorary blueberry. People from the Saguenay– Lac-Saint-Jean region around Chicoutimi are known as *bleuets*, and to be an honorary blueberry, even if it was purely an arbitrary notion of Tremblay's, was gratifying.

After a few years, Tremblay used the knowledge he'd acquired while covering the Canadiens to start writing a script for a soap opera, using as a backdrop a professional hockey team. The series burst onto the TV screens in 1986 as one of the most popular shows in Quebec history—*Lance et Compte*. An English version—*He Shoots, He Scores*—was subsequently popular on English-language TV.

After *Lance et Compte* had run its course, Tremblay wrote a new series. This one was *Scoop*, based on the tumultuous world of newspapers.

There were a number of other scripts after that, and in 2002, 2004 and 2006, "new generation" versions of *Lance et Compte* hit Quebec television.

Not bad for a guy who couldn't figure out how to use an electric blanket.

TEN
Enforcers

In the hockey world, the widely accepted wisdom regarding scouts is that they spend too much time talking to each other. Whether this is true or not, I couldn't say. I do know that when they gather in the press room before a game, they all sit at the same table. And I know that when they're scouting junior games, they tend to congregate in the same part of the rink.

But I also know that these guys are the most exploited section of any hockey team's organization. They're not paid much. They're away from their families a lot. The team's view of their allowable expenses is far from liberal. Their travel is rarely luxurious and their job security is non-existent.

Scouts can be found driving the back roads during a Canadian blizzard and trying to stay warm in cheap motels and eating short-order meals at truck stops. In the better organizations, the more respected scouts are treated well. But such situations are far from the norm.

If a coach can't get a hot prospect to live up to his potential, or if a general manager needlessly creates an atmosphere of animosity in contract negotiations, or if teammates take a dislike to the youngster and make him uncomfortable, it's not necessarily the coach or the GM or the other players who get the blame. It's the scout who wanted to draft him.

Granted, some players slip through the scouts' net. Luc Robitaille, for instance, has been inducted into the Hall of Fame, but he was drafted 171st. Curtis Joseph, who may be in the Hall of Fame some day, wasn't drafted at all. Ditto for Ed Belfour.

But it's no accident that the teams who make their scouts an integral part of the organization reap the benefits year after year.

It has become a mantra for fans to chant that a team must have high draft picks to be successful. Such a statement is totally inaccurate, but it rarely gets challenged. The next time someone tells you that a team can't win without high draft picks, ask that person which team has won the most Stanley Cups in the past fifteen years. The answer is the Detroit Red Wings.

And which team has had the fewest first-round draft picks—and no high ones at all—in the last fifteen years? The answer is the Detroit Red Wings.

In fact, over the last twenty years, the Red Wings have had only one pick in the top ten. That was Martin Lapointe, whom they drafted 10th in 1991. Their next highest selection was Jakob Kindl drafted 19th in 2005.

The truth is that the team has to make sure that it uses its draft picks to maximum advantage. They don't necessarily have to be high picks.

The Wings value their scouts. They pay them well and they treat them properly. As a result, they can draft people like Nick Lidstrom (53rd), Johan Franzen (97th), Henrik

Zetterberg (210th), Jimmy Howard (64th), Jiri Hudler (58th), Valtteri Filppula (95th) and Tomas Holmstrom (257th).

But the Wings are the exception. Most teams pay their scouts poorly. And get what they pay for.

•   •   •

One of the best players ever to escape the scouts' attention was Doug Gilmour and there was absolutely no excuse for it.

It wasn't as if Gilmour was playing for some tractor-dealership team in Siberia or a Tier III team in Labrador. He was playing for the Cornwall Royals, often alongside the guy who was a consensus number-one pick at the time, Dale Hawerchuk.

The Winnipeg Jets, who were in the process of earning themselves the first selection, watched Hawerchuk play no fewer than sixty-three times in the 1980–81 season, but didn't bother to draft Gilmour. Still, the Jets can't be singled out for blame. They weren't the only ones who ignored him.

Gilmour went through the entire draft in his first year of eligibility. All the scouts agreed he was too slight for the NHL, even though in the Memorial Cup tournament, he was often the best player on the ice for the Royals.

The next year, as an overage player, Gilmour led the Ontario Hockey League (OHL) in scoring with 177 points. All the scouts agreed he was too old.

It was not until the seventh round (134th overall) that Ron Caron, then the general manager of the St. Louis Blues, decided to take a chance on him. And that was largely because the Blues, who were under strict financial limitations at the time, knew that Gilmour would come cheaply. The Blues thought he might develop into a decent defensive player.

He did. He also developed into a great offensive player. He even played for Team Canada in the 1987 Canada Cup. And by then, the scouts had agreed that he was no longer too small or too old.

• • •

In November 1985, Philadelphia Flyers goalie Pelle Lindbergh was killed on his way home from a bar. Like many pro athletes, he had a fast car, a Porsche in his case. Heading around a bend at a high rate of speed, the car failed to make the turn and slammed into a wall.

The media moralizers, who never miss an opportunity to preach, quickly jumped into print with sermons on the dangers of drinking and driving.

Certainly those dangers exist, but they weren't to blame in this case. Lindbergh had always been a heavy drinker. His hockey coach back in Sweden said that Lindbergh had been combining drinking and driving without any ill effects since he was fifteen. He possessed catlike reflexes and refused to be convinced that they were affected to any serious level by alcohol.

There is still no evidence that he was wrong. On the night he died, Lindbergh left the bar with two friends, one male, one female. With the car being a two-seater, the man sat in the passenger seat.

The woman scrunched into the space between the seats.

Even though Lindbergh had great faith in his ability to drive after drinking, his female passenger didn't share it. She repeatedly told him to slow down and when he didn't, she turned off the ignition.

In a Porsche, two important things happen when you

turn off the ignition. One is that the engine dies. The other is that the steering locks. Lindbergh could handle a dying engine, but with the steering locked, he couldn't turn. The car went directly into the wall. Lindberg was critically injured and died in hospital.

The passengers were also injured but both lived.

So did part of the car. Baseball star Pete Rose bought the engine, which was undamaged since the Porsche is a rear-engine car, and had it installed in his own Porsche.

• • •

When he played for the Los Angeles Kings in their days of purple-and-yellow uniforms prior to 1988, Kenny Baumgartner was never afraid to show his true colours. He dyed his previously blond hair purple and yellow.

To begin the game, he would come running out of the dressing room, race down the corridor and vault the boards.

On some nights, this was just about the only ice time that Kenny saw. He was an enforcer who took a conscientious approach to his job, and game misconducts were certainly not a rarity in his career.

Should a scrum start, Kenny liked nothing better than to wade in, shouting, "Daddy's home," in an ominous singsong tone.

One such night, the Kings were playing the Calgary Flames, who had a new kid in the lineup, Theoren Fleury. A full-scale melee developed—which was no surprise since the Kings of the 1988–89 season not only had Baumgartner on the team, they also had Jay Miller and Marty McSorley.

Wayne Gretzky grabbed Fleury and said, "Stay here with me, kid. We don't need to be in there."

Fleury, a little pepper pot, said, "No way," wrenched free of Gretzky's grasp and charged into the fray. Baumgartner, who was busy with someone else, saw him coming, reached out and popped him on the nose. Then he returned to his previous engagement.

Fleury, blood streaming from his nose, staggered back to Gretzky, who said, "You want to stay here with me now?"

• • •

To the average fan, Kenny Baumgartner appeared to be almost a caricature of an NHL enforcer. But really, he was nothing of the sort.

He used a Sher-Wood stick and opted for the model that was decorated with three strips of red adhesive plastic tape near the blade. One day, he was sitting in the dressing room with a razor blade, shaving off the red rings.

"What are you doing that for?" I asked.

"Aesthetic purposes," replied Kenny.

Not quite the reply one would expect from an NHL enforcer.

But perhaps Kenny's most eloquent observation came during the 1995 lockout. He was a member of the executive committee of the National Hockey League Players' Association and, as such, was occasionally approached for comment by the media.

At this point in the lockout, the NHL had been hinting that if the matter weren't resolved soon, it might consider using replacement players, and that some of them might be allowed to stay on a team's roster when the players went back to work.

Baumgartner was asked if he thought these players might be able to hang on to a post-lockout job.

"Perhaps they could," he said. "But they'd have to remember that hockey is a game which lends itself very well to retribution."

• • •

Gino Odjick had already established himself as an NHL enforcer with the Vancouver Canucks when his buddy Sandy McCarthy attended his first training camp with the Calgary Flames.

McCarthy wanted to win a job as the Flames' policeman, but in a pre-season game, Odjick was roaming around, running Calgary players into the boards and generally creating mayhem.

McCarthy lined up next to Odjick for a faceoff and said, "Come on, Gino. Take it easy. You're making me look bad. If you keep doing that, they're going to want me to fight you."

"Don't worry about it, Sandy," said Odjick. "Do what you've got to do."

At that point, the gloves came off and the two staged what turned out to be one of the best fights of the season. They were both tough guys and each landed a number of heavy shots.

After the game, I was in the hallway outside the visiting team's dressing room when McCarthy came up. Even though protocol is somewhat relaxed during the pre-season, there was no way that McCarthy could go into the Canucks' room. So he asked me to do it for him.

"Would you tell Gino I'm waiting for him and ask him to hurry up?"

They were going out for pizza together and McCarthy was hungry.

• • •

Sergei Zholtok was never a great player in the National Hockey League, but he was solid and he spent ten years in the league, which was no mean feat.

He was also one of a select few professionals who played for two national teams. In international hockey, once you declare a team, even if you do so at the junior level, it's very difficult to get permission to change allegiances.

Sergei was born in the Latvian Soviet Socialist Republic and when the Iron Curtain was in place, he played for the Soviet Union. But after the collapse of that empire, Latvia regained its sovereignty and Sergei was the undisputed star of the Latvian team.

He always seemed to be smiling, so whenever our paths crossed, I'd chat with him. We had a mutual friend in Oleg Tverdovsky, who had left the NHL to play in Omsk, and we were talking about him one day.

I suggested that spending time in Omsk, which is in Siberia and 2700 kilometres east of Moscow, would not be my idea of a good time, especially in winter. The average temperature in January is in the minus 20-degree Celsius range.

Sergei, who had been there, said that it was a bleak place, something of a cultural backwater and that the winters bordered on the unbearable.

"I can't imagine what that would be like," I said.

Sergei quickly enlightened me. "It would be like Edmonton," he said with a laugh.

• • •

Sergei Zholtok was only thirty-one when he died in 2004.

His NHL career had ended the year before, and he was back home, playing for Riga 2000 in a game against Dynamo Minsk in Belarus.

While he was in the NHL, he had occasionally exhibited some health problems. He had experienced occasional dizziness and sometimes felt fatigued, but with the demanding lifestyle of an NHL player being what it is, symptoms of that nature are not terribly unusual.

In January 2003, while playing for the Minnesota Wild, he was diagnosed with cardiac arrhythmia, an irregular heartbeat, and was hospitalized overnight. He missed seven games but the problem was deemed to be under control.

He played most of the game against Minsk but left with about five minutes remaining and went into the dressing room.

When his teammates came in after the game, he was dead on the floor.

• • •

It is possible—in fact, likely—that if he had been able to enjoy a full career, Pavel Bure would have been the greatest Russian hockey player in history.

Perhaps he would have been to forwards what Bobby Orr was to defencemen. But as was the case with Orr, Bure was driven out of the game by injuries long before his talent had deserted him.

At least Orr had the satisfaction of knowing that he was revered by the organization for which he played most of his career. That was never the case with Bure.

Bure did not leave the Vancouver Canucks because the

relationship turned bad. He left because the relationship had always been bad.

The Canucks drafted him under cloudy circumstances. Even today, many hockey executives feel that the documents that the Canucks used to establish Bure's legitimacy as a 1989 draft choice were somewhat spurious. The debate raged long after draft day.

Nevertheless, penniless and unsure of his status, Bure left the Soviet Union in time to join the team for its 1989 training camp and told the Canucks he was off to Los Angeles where he would be staying at his agent's house, awaiting the arrival of someone from the team.

"Then it took two weeks before somebody showed up," he said. He had no equipment and no money to buy any.

"It was really hard," he said. "I thought they would be waiting for me when I got there. But there was nobody."

Finally, Brian Burke, then assistant to Canucks general manager Pat Quinn, arrived. "We just had a quick lunch and I didn't see them again for another ten days," Bure said. "I was nervous. I was young."

Burke subsequently arranged a court hearing in Detroit to get Bure's release from the Red Army, which had owned his Soviet rights. The cost of that release was $250,000. The Canucks paid $200,000 and told Bure he had to pay the other $50,000.

The day before the court judgment, Bure agreed to an NHL contract worth $600,000 annually. But there was an understanding, he said, that if he proved he was a solid NHL player, a new deal would be written.

He scored 34 goals that season and won the Calder Trophy as the NHL's best rookie, even though he missed seventeen games, mostly while awaiting the court's decision.

He then asked about the new deal he had been promised. "They said, 'Hold on, you have to play a little bit more. You have to prove it to us,'" Bure said.

So he played another year. This time he scored 60 goals. The team's response?

"They said, 'Okay, let us think about it.'"

They thought about it during the summer and finally made an offer—$14.7 million over five years.

Bure was thrilled. Now his salary appeared to be in line with what was being paid to his two Soviet linemates in the World Junior Championship, Alex Mogilny and Sergei Fedorov.

But when he went to sign the deal, the Canucks revealed the small print. They wanted to pay him in Canadian dollars, which in those days were worth about 85 cents U.S. Bure refused to sign.

He and his agent decided that the best course of action would be for Bure to go to training camp while the two sides worked on a new contract.

When the season started, negotiations were still dragging on. Two months into the season, Bure was off to a slow start, and now the Canucks said they were having second thoughts.

As Bure explained it, "I asked for a trade in '93 because they said, 'Well, you can't play any more. You got 60 goals, but you just got lucky. You'll be lucky to get 30 goals again.'

"I said, 'Okay. You don't trust me. Then trade me.'"

He had had enough. But he didn't sulk. He played well and despite the shaky start, still managed to produce another 60-goal season. He even led the Canucks to the Stanley

Cup final, which they lost in seven games to the New York Rangers. While the playoffs were going on, the Canucks, now apparently finally aware that Bure was a player of value, offered him a large contract.

Bure wanted to stick to his guns. As he explained it, "I said, 'Listen, I asked for a trade. Don't sign me. Just trade me.'"

But his agent urged him to settle, and so he did. The cost to the Canucks was enormous. In fact, it cost the team more than twice as much as the deal Bure would willingly have signed eight months earlier. Now, the average salary was in the US$5-million range. Also, there were astonishing bonus clauses that gave him an extra $3.5 million in the first year.

Once again, the Canucks had played hardball and lost.

• • •

By this time, the relationship should have survived its rocky start. The Canucks should have recognized Bure's value and acted accordingly. Not a chance.

When the time came to put pen to paper, Quinn made it clear he wanted no part of such a precedent-setting contract, which had been forced upon him by ownership. However, Bure refused to sign the deal until Quinn was summoned to the room and shook his hand.

By that time, allegations had surfaced in a number of media outlets that Bure had threatened to quit the team unless he got his deal. "That really pissed me off," he said. "That's a lie."

He's certain someone in the Vancouver organization spread that story, but he doesn't know who it was. "And I don't want to say what I don't know," he added. "But I know one thing. I was promised to be traded."

That contract carried a signing bonus to be paid immediately. It was not until four months later that Bure received it.

Then came the lockout. Having realized a labour disruption was likely, his agent had insisted on ironclad guarantees that Bure would be paid whether the league operated or not. Nevertheless, the Canucks refused to pay.

It was not until October 1997 that Bure got his payment for that part of the 1994–95 season. And even then, it was a settlement, not full payment. To save legal fees—not to mention the acrimony that would have been caused by suing the club for which he played—Bure settled for $1 million of the $1.7 million he was owed.

• • •

While all this was going on, Bure was still playing hard. And still getting hurt. He played only fifteen games in the 1995–96 season.

He had a series of knee injuries and suffered from recurring back problems. Although he played sixty-three of the eighty-two games in the 1996–97 season, his heart was not with the Canucks. He had never felt valued, and no one at management level had ever given him any reason to change that opinion.

"So at the end of 1996–97, I went to see Pat [Quinn] and I said, 'I'm getting too many injuries with my knee and my back. It's time to move me on. Maybe if I go somewhere else, I'm going to play with more emotion and it's going to stretch me out and maybe I'll play better.'

"He said, 'If you really want that, we'll trade you. I understand that's what you want.' That was '97. Then I waited all of '97 and '98."

By that time, Quinn had moved on and Brian Burke had become the Canucks' GM. When he still hadn't been moved by the start of the Canucks 1998 training camp, Bure walked out.

During a news conference to bring the media up to date on developments, Burke was asked what prompted Bure's actions. He professed not to know.

ELEVEN

A Gretzky deal and other strange encounters

Wayne Gretzky has a number of corporate affiliations. Essentially, these companies buy his time. A certain number of his days per annum belong to them and they can designate them as they choose.

They may want Gretzky to play in a golf tournament. They may want him to make a series of promotional appearances as their representative. They may want him to meet the company's brass or attend a series of meetings.

On the days when he is going to a series of functions—which is often—Gretzky will sign two hundred glossy photos before breakfast because he knows from experience that a strict schedule is imposed for each appearance on days like this and he'll run out of time before everyone gets an autograph. So he takes extras.

In the limo on the way, he'll usually sign some more. When he arrives, the organizers invariably have more items for him to sign. After the formal proceedings, he'll often sit for an hour signing more autographs.

On one such day when I was with him, he figured that by midafternoon, he had signed 1700 autographs that day. And he still had to go to Las Vegas for a charity event that night where he would probably do another three hundred or so.

This was an inordinately high number for one day, but even so, Gretzky believes that he signs at least 75,000 autographs a year. And some people still get turned down.

"You can't answer everything that comes in the mail," he says. "There aren't enough hours in the day. What I try to do is get things signed for charity events or if kids are sick in hospital. It's a full-time job."

And then there are the casual autographs when he's out in public.

"It's hard sometimes because when you become somebody, you're not supposed to have bad days, you're not supposed to not feel great," he says. "There are times when I'm tired or I'm not feeling great and people walk away and say, 'Oh, he wasn't that nice.' People sometimes forget that you're human. But in general, you try to be yourself.

"I was with a guy once who doesn't sign autographs. I was shocked. If the same person comes back for the eighth time with the twenty-third card he wants signed, I might say, 'Okay, you've had enough,' but this guy wouldn't sign any— and he's well known. It blew me away.

"Then a little while after he left, his daughter came back to me and said, 'Would you sign this for my dad?'

"Autographs don't bother me one bit, but I would never ask anybody for an autograph. I'd get a little nervous about that.

"It used to be 'You're my favourite player. Will you sign this picture?' Now they send you a note saying, 'You're my favourite player,' along with sixteen cards. The whole collectors thing is out of control."

•   •   •

On Long Island, NHL teams tend to stay at the Marriott, which is right across the parking lot from the Nassau Veterans Memorial Coliseum.

Autograph hunters know this, so in the late mornings, when visiting players are walking back and forth between the hotel and the morning skate, they station themselves in the parking lot and await their opportunities.

Gretzky and I were walking back from the rink one morning when a group of three teenagers came up and asked him for autographs. They each had a number of cards, but he signed them all, then we continued to walk.

When we were about twenty yards away, we heard the kids shout in unison, "Gretzky sucks."

He just laughed.

• • •

The Montreal Canadiens always used to go on an extended west coast road trip in early December. GM Sam Pollock believed that people would be less likely to buy hockey tickets in December, so we'd be on the road for at least ten days.

On one of these trips, the team played in Los Angeles and was to fly to Vancouver the next morning. We were staying at an airport hotel and someone noticed that until midnight, there were cheap flights every thirty minutes from L.A. to Las Vegas. Right after the game, we could scoot over, then fly back in the early morning and connect to the outgoing plane to Vancouver.

There were no players in this entourage, just some reporters and a few of the hangers-on who travelled with the team.

It was the first time I had ever been in Las Vegas and I

had a run of beginner's luck. I came away $600 to the good, which was about three weeks' salary for a sportswriter in 1974.

When we got to Vancouver, I used some of the money to splurge on a flashy outfit—a black three-piece suit made of either velvet or velour or velveteen, or some such fabric. Fabric is not my area of expertise, but I'm sure you know what I mean. Short, fuzzy stuff. In my defence, I submit two mitigating circumstances: (1) It was the seventies; (2) I admired Don Cherry.

For the game in Vancouver, I was down at the rink early, hanging around the dressing room in my flashy black velvet or velour or velveteen three-piece suit. Sportswriters are not exactly famous for their haberdashery—well, not in a good sense—so my arrival caused quite a stir. A few comments were made and a couple of the players even gave me a congratulatory pat on the back.

It was not until some time later, when I'd gone up to the press room, that it was pointed out that it might be a good idea to get all that talcum powder off the back of my jacket.

• • •

For years, the Madison Pub was the place to go in Toronto if you wanted to meet NHL players.

It started to get that reputation during the late eighties when Wendel Clark moved to 100 Madison Avenue, in a house owned by hockey agent Don Meehan.

It was an old Georgian-style house—basically square frontage—divided into four large apartments. The two lower ones had most of their living space on the main floor, but they also had large finished basements. The two upper ones had their living areas on the second floor of the house and bedrooms on the third floors.

Meehan himself lived in the upper right apartment. Wendel was in the upper left. Those two apartments shared a huge balcony outside their back doors—a balcony that had a hot tub in one corner. During the Leafs' 1993 playoff run that took the team to the Stanley Cup semifinal, that balcony was the scene of huge parties after many of the home games.

Clark got married and left shortly after that season, but over the years, a number of other Leafs lived in the building. Alyn McCauley rented Clark's former apartment at the same time as teammate Kevyn Adams was in the lower right. I lived in the lower left from 1996 to 2007, having taken over from Kent Manderville. Goalie Damien Rhodes lived there for a while too. The late Peter Zezel was a tenant during some of his Leafs years. TSN broadcaster Gord Miller lived in the building for a while.

Sometimes, some of the other Meehan clients who were awaiting assignment or sitting out in a contract dispute stayed there. Travis Green was one of them. Oleg Tverdovsky was another. So was the Leafs 1999 first-round draft pick, Luca Cereda.

The people in the neighbourhood knew the place and so did the kids. Wendel wasn't far from being a kid himself and he used to play road hockey in front of the house.

In the evenings, some or all of the tenants of 100 Madison would often walk down to the Madison Pub, which occupied three Victorian houses at numbers 14, 16 and 18. That was the beginning of the pub's mystique and its status as Toronto's hockey pub.

• • •

Nowadays, NHL teams invariably rush out of the arena after the game to grab their charter flight for home—or for the next city on the road trip.

But in the eighties, and even well into the nineties, most NHL teams used commercial flights and left town the morning after the game.

Don Meehan had more NHL clients than any other agent, and as often as not, those clients would meet him in the Madison Pub after the game. Often, they'd bring along a few teammates. As a result, on many game nights, most of the players who had been on the ice at Maple Leaf Gardens a couple of hours earlier could be found at the Madison until closing time.

The Russians were rarely there. Russians love to eat a large meal after a game, and while the Madison had a good pub menu, it did not provide the kind of fare the Russians wanted. But players of every other nationality called in at the Madison with great regularity.

On other occasions—GM meetings, Hall of Fame inductions and so on—the Madison was again the pub of choice.

Most NHL vice-presidents have been in the place, but no commissioners. Gary Bettman refused to come along on a Hall of Fame night when I assured him that a number of his vice-presidents would be there, which they were. Most general managers have been in it, as have a host of other high-ranking staffers: personnel directors, head scouts, public-relations directors, coaches, assistant coaches and many others. The executive head of the NHL Players' Association, Bob Goodenow, was a frequent visitor.

The Madison isn't really a hockey pub anymore. The NHL's switch to charter flights killed that. The players are too disciplined to go out the night before a game, and they don't stay overnight after one.

In 2007, Don Meehan sold his house and moved to Oakville. The Madison is still an excellent pub—but not in the way it used to be.

•   •   •

I lived in Calgary for six years keeping track of western Canadian sports for the *Globe and Mail*, so even though most of my responsibilities had to do with hockey, there were also other sports that needed covering—mostly football, baseball and skiing.

The CBC also covered skiing and accordingly sent out Brian Williams, one of their premier sports announcers, for a major World Cup race.

Brian was born in Winnipeg and for years lived in Invermere, British Columbia, about two hours from Lake Louise, so he grew up skiing. On this day, he didn't have his skis or boots with him, but he wanted to study the course, so he took the chairlift to the top and was wandering around, peering down the slope to see what the skiers had to encounter. He was also leaving large footprints in the snow.

Dave Irwin was up there as well, hanging out with his friends in the ski fraternity. Irwin was not only one of the Crazy Canucks, he was widely conceded to be the craziest.

Irwin is not very tall, but he's built like a fire plug. And for a guy who had made his living as a professional downhill skier, risking his life on every run, he was astonishingly easygoing.

To him, it seemed odd that someone should be at the top of a ski hill with no skis on. He knew Brian, who had often covered the Crazy Canucks in their heyday, and since the two were going to be working together on the telecast, he offered to save Williams the bother of going back down on the lift.

"Just climb on my back," he said. "I'll take you down."

Williams wasn't sure that he was serious.

"Really," said Irwin. "Just be a sack of potatoes up there. Don't be leaning one way or the other or trying to make the turns. I'll do all that. You just sit there."

Williams climbed up and off they went—piggyback down the men's downhill run, which is not exactly the bunny slope.

For the first few moments, Williams was terrified. But he soon realized that Irwin had the run totally under control. He took a couple of bumps easily and made a couple of turns.

Then he turned around and started going down backwards. Brian's terror returned.

"See up there?" asked Irwin pointing back up the hill. "That's where the skiers have to make a sharp turn but they can't go too wide."

And so it went. Irwin skied the men's downhill with Williams on his back, pointing out the finer points of the race as he went—sometimes backwards.

If you ever run into Brian Williams, ask him about skiing downhill with Dave Irwin. He still gets goosebumps when he talks about it.

● ● ●

The NHL's Canadian teams like to pretend that they're the saviours of hockey, the people who put the game before money, the heritage before the marketing. Unfortunately, none of it is true.

Whether or not you think Wayne Gretzky is the greatest player of all time, you'd probably have to concede that in 1996, his was the greatest name in hockey. Yet he was a free agent who had to go to the United States to find a place to exhibit his talent.

The Calgary Flames, Edmonton Oilers and Ottawa Senators were all facing serious financial concerns in those days. They didn't want him. The Montreal Canadiens prefer their stars to be French-Canadian.

That left the Toronto Maple Leafs and Vancouver Canucks.

Gretzky was leaning towards a return to Canada and let it be known that he would have no objection to playing for Vancouver, but the general manager of the day, Pat Quinn, said he had no interest in such an eventuality and departed for a vacation in the Far East.

He should have checked with the team owner, John McCaw—an American. When McCaw found out that Gretzky was willing to play for his Canucks, he was thrilled and called Quinn back from his vacation.

The logistics of the negotiations were unusual, to say the least. They started in the morning, and in one room, Gretzky's agent and lawyer were trying to hammer out a contract with Quinn, Canucks assistant GM George McPhee and team accountants.

Meanwhile, in an adjacent room, Gretzky and McCaw chatted, relaxed, shared reminiscences and generally set the foundation for a firm friendship.

Late in the evening, with negotiations still dragging on,

those two decided that they'd hung around long enough. McCaw went his way and Gretzky went back to his hotel room.

In the wee hours, the phone rang. A deal had been reached. Gretzky had to return to the offices and sign it immediately.

Gretzky refused. He would give his word that he would sign the deal as it stood in the morning, but he had no intention of trooping back to the office at 2 a.m. for the formality of signing a deal that he had accepted.

That wasn't good enough. "It's now or never" was the response.

"That's up to you," said Gretzky.

No doubt the Canucks management felt that Gretzky was trying to use their offer as leverage. That was simply not true. Either way, Gretzky was lost to the Canucks. When McCaw found out, he was furious, and Quinn was on the slippery slope. Because the Canucks didn't sign Gretzky and McCaw wanted a big name, they next went after Mark Messier. They got him, but the contract cost $20 million, considerably more than the proposed Gretzky deal, and Messier's tenure was something less than a resounding success.

In November 1997, McCaw fired Quinn.

• • •

The Maple Leafs' turn came next. Ever since he was a boy, Gretzky had wanted to play for the Leafs, the team he grew up following.

Cliff Fletcher was the Leafs' GM at the time and he would have loved to grant Gretzky's wish.

"There were four deals I could have had," said Gretzky in

a 2009 interview. "Bob Gainey called from the Dallas Stars, but I felt I'd already played in the southern United States and I didn't want to do that again. At that time, Dallas wasn't as established as it became later. Bob gave me a firm offer, and it was a good deal, but I'd been through the thing of building a team in the South and I just wanted to go to a team that was more established.

"The second offer was from Vancouver. I spent fourteen hours negotiating with them, but that fell through. I was really kind of relieved because I really wanted to go to Toronto.

"We called Cliff [Fletcher] and asked if he was interested. He said he was, but if I was looking for big money, it was not going to happen. The owner was trying to save money to put it towards a new arena.

"So I said, 'Just put together a reasonable offer and we'll see what we can do.'

"He came back with a deal for $3 million a year with some money deferred. We said, 'Okay, we like that.'

"Toronto was my first choice. It was really where I wanted to go. But Cliff came back and said he had taken it to the owner and the owner nixed it."

When Fletcher got the Gretzky commitment, he was ecstatic and he quickly took the deal to Leafs owner Steve Stavro for what he thought would be immediate approval. Instead, Stavro's response was "How many seats will that sell?"

The answer, of course, was that it wouldn't sell any. The Leafs sold out every game. Gretzky was not to become a Maple Leaf.

The next day, the New York Rangers made an offer and Canada's greatest player wound up his career in the United States.

• • •

Perhaps the worst thing ever to happen to Peter Mahovlich was the magnificent goal he scored for Team Canada in the 1972 Super Series against the Soviet Union. After that, fans expected him to score end-to-end goals like that every night.

He did score a lot of goals. In fact, in the 1974–75 season, as part of the Montreal Canadiens dynasty, he got 35 of them, and, thanks to excellent seasons from linemates Guy Lafleur and Steve Shutt, added 82 assists. That 117-point season was the apex of his career.

Lafleur and Shutt liked to operate at full speed in a straight line, but Mahovlich was more inclined to take a circular path to the net and rarely got into top gear. As a result, Shutt started referring to the trio as the "Donut Line." When I looked at him quizzically, he explained: "No centre."

When Pete was taken off the top line and replaced by Jacques Lemaire, it was the beginning of the end for Mahovlich in Montreal. In 1977, he was traded to Pittsburgh. But he left behind a legacy of Mahovlich moments.

• • •

One such moment came when Continental Airlines decided to promote its red-eye flights from Los Angeles to Chicago by offering 5-cent beers.

In that pre-charter era, the Canadiens always wound up their west coast swings by taking the late-night flight to Chicago, arriving around 3 a.m., then taking the first flight to Montreal, which left around 6 a.m.

When we boarded the flight to Chicago, Mahovlich

approached the stewardess (they hadn't yet become "flight attendants"). "When can we get the 5-cent beers?" he asked.

"As soon as the pilot turns off the seat-belt sign, sir. How many do you want?"

"All of them," said Mahovlich.

"You can't have all of them," said the stewardess.

"Why not?" asked Mahovlich. "The beers are for sale and I want to buy them. What's the problem?"

"You can't take them off the plane."

"I won't take them off the plane. Don't worry. My friends will make sure there aren't any left by the time we get to Chicago."

Pete got his beers, and we made sure he was able to keep his promise.

• • •

On another flight, this one in late afternoon, the stewardess was serving dinner and accidentally dropped the meal into Pete's lap.

She rushed off, came back with some towels and offered them to Pete. "Here, sir," she said. "You can wipe it up with this. I'm so sorry."

"You wipe it up," said Pete. "You spilled it. You wipe it up."

The stewardess started to turn red. "I can't do that," she said.

"But you're the one who spilled it," said Pete. "You should be the one who wipes it up."

By this time, everyone within three rows knew what was happening and took up Pete's case. The stewardess was clearly getting flustered, and the guys on the team were chortling loudly.

Pete liked to have fun, but he was never a bully. When he

saw that the woman was starting to get upset, he conceded
the point and cleaned up his own lap.

• • •

Another stewardess wasn't as lucky. Pete started goofing
around with her—I can't remember now what his point was,
but I doubt very much that it had any merit—and she started
snapping back at him.

She was a tiny woman, but clearly one of those people of
either gender who have a Napoleon complex. Not only was
she not going to go along with Pete's tomfoolery, she was doing
everything she could to belittle him in front of his teammates.

The confrontation went on for a while, then Pete decided
he'd had enough. Unwinding his six-four frame from his
seat, he moved out into the aisle, picked up the stewardess
and shoved her into the luggage rack. She shouted furiously,
but to no avail. Into the luggage rack she went.

Unfortunately for Pete, who rarely took anything
seriously, she was of a totally different disposition. She filed a
complaint with the team and a few days later Pete got reamed
out by a very unhappy Sam Pollock.

• • •

In 1975, one of the years in which the Canadiens were
dominating the NHL, the all-star game was in Philadelphia.

The Canadiens had eight players on the all-star team,
and their next NHL game was on the road, so Scott Bowman
made arrangements for the Montreal players to practise on
their own at the Spectrum on the morning after the all-star
game. As usual, the travelling press showed up for the skate,
and someone on the team suggested that since there were

only eight players on the ice, we should come out and skate with them.

The lack of equipment was a problem that could be solved by the fact that the Atlanta Flames were to play in Philly that night. Their equipment was already in the visiting team's dressing room. We might have had permission to help ourselves, but I doubt it.

Tom Lysiak was about my size, so I borrowed his gear and headed onto the ice.

Ken Dryden was in goal and the guys were taking turns going in for shots. A couple of the other reporters did it and were stopped by Dryden.

When it was my turn, I started heading in. Dryden took one look, vacated the net and skated towards the corner.

"What are you doing?" I asked.

"The chances of you scoring on me are so infinitesimal as to be virtually non-existent," he said. "However, if by some monumental fluke of nature, you should happen to put one in the net, I know I would hear about it for the rest of my life. You're not going to get that chance."

So I put it in the empty net. As far as I was concerned, Dryden was the goalie of record.

• • •

In those days, Dryden was often a lot of fun and certainly aware of the responsibilities of a professional athlete.

His stall in the Forum dressing room was the first on the left as you came in the door, so it made sense to stop there first after a game. And he was always available. Many players were only too happy to talk to reporters after a win but couldn't be found with the Hubble Telescope after a loss.

I didn't have a lot of social graces in those days—many would say there hasn't been much evolution on that front—so I usually just asked what I wanted to know without bothering to preface it with a bunch of flattery.

Or sometimes, I'd be sarcastic. "You know that sliding shot from the point that got past you, Kenny? Were the guys on the other team screaming, 'Sweep, sweep'?"

After he lost 4–1 to the New York Rangers in the first game of the 1977 Stanley Cup final, he was sitting with his head down, surrounded by reporters, none of whom wanted to break the ice.

"Any chance of an improvement next game, Kenny?" I asked.

Dryden looked up. "When you die," he said, "they're going to put on your tombstone that you expired of terminal flippancy."

But he did answer all the questions.

Somehow, though, in his later years, he began to get a bit full of himself. Perhaps that's what life at the government trough does for you.

Even before he was elected as a Liberal MP, he had been a part of various commissions and studies at the taxpayers' expense.

I wasn't the only one who noticed his condescending attitude.

In 1999, when he was representing the Maple Leafs at the annual meeting of NHL general managers, he skipped the golf game that most of them were enjoying one afternoon and opted to go for a hot-air-balloon ride instead.

When told of this, one of his fellow GMs responded quickly.

"Did he need a balloon?" he asked.

• • •

The scene at the Madison Pub was such that we always hung around the same area, and various visitors would come and go. One night, Brian Stemmle wandered over.

Stemmle was a great downhill skier, but he suffered a number of serious falls, the most horrific coming at Kitzbühel, Austria, in 1989. That one nearly killed him.

In fact, the doctors told him that had the accident happened five years earlier, he would definitely not have survived. Only the most up-to-date advances in medical technology kept him alive.

I'd skied with Stemmle a bit, and we had a number of mutual friends, so we were having a pleasant chat when Mike Zeisberger, of the *Toronto Sun*, joined the group.

The conversation continued, as is often the case at times like this, without any introductions, until I finally realized Zeis wasn't aware who Stemmle was. I said, "Zeis, have you met Brian Stemmle?"

"Oh, sorry," said Zeis. "I didn't recognize you not hanging from a helicopter."

Stemmle thought that was a good line.

TWELVE
Dis-honoured at the Hall

I knew Sgt. Al Probert long before I knew his son Bob, and
I must admit that I never liked him. When I was attending
the University of Windsor in the sixties, Big Al, a Windsor
cop, had seized my car saying it was unsafe. It may have
been—well, let's face it, it was—but I disliked him anyway
and the feeling was mutual.

I got along with a lot of the Windsor cops, but Probert
rented himself out to provide security at the University of
Windsor Lancers' home hockey games. I rarely missed
one, and we didn't always see eye to eye on what was—and
was not—proper conduct for a fan. In retrospect, his ideas
probably had more merit than mine. After all, as a university student I knew everything there was to know in the
world.

Big Al was one of those intense, humourless guys who
made it clear through his glares and his actions that he
thoroughly disapproved of you. Bob was not at all like his
father. He was much more easy-going and never seemed to
be overly concerned about the troubles in which he found
himself, which were numerous.

Growing up with Big Al as a father couldn't have been

easy. Bob had a brother, Norm, and Big Al would occasionally come home with a present for his son.

Which one? That was up to the boys to determine. He'd place the present on the floor and tell them to fight for it.

No wonder Bob became as feared a fighter as there was in the National Hockey League. Yet to me—and to every other media person as far as I know—he was never anything but friendly and cooperative.

One time, during one of his suspensions, we were outside the Red Wings dressing room having a long chat about the usual hockey things. He sat there, in his underwear, relaxed and drawing on his cigarette, a ready smile displaying his lack of front teeth. He looked like anything but an enforcer.

He was a huge fan favourite in Detroit, and one of the best-selling items at the Red Wings store in the Joe Louis Arena was a T-shirt with "Give Blood" written across the chest. Underneath that was a large red cross. And underneath that, "Fight Probert."

He played 16 seasons—or parts thereof when he wasn't suspended—and he racked up 3300 penalty minutes. But he was much more than just a dancing bear. He also had 179 goals and 253 assists.

On July 5, 2010, Bob Probert collapsed on his boat and died. He was forty-five.

• • •

In a way, there is a media wing to the Hockey Hall of Fame. To me, it doesn't make an awful lot of sense. Hockey fans don't go to the Hall of Fame to see plaques glorifying sportswriters, especially since, in many cases, the honour is bestowed for nothing more than longevity.

If you cover hockey in Toronto long enough, they'll put you in the media wing of the Hall of Fame, even though you might be a notorious homer, a functional illiterate or a plagiarist. Or, as in some well documented cases, all three.

But many people disagree with me and see media inclusion as a function of the Hall, especially in view of the 2010 decision to include women. As one person suggested, "If they're going to let women in, they should also consider the 100,000 boys who play midget hockey. It's the same level of expertise."

Yet even among the people who support full Hall of Fame membership for the media, there has been a major dispute about the manner in which this should be effected. Red Fisher of the *Montreal Gazette* says he worked out the terms of induction with Clarence Campbell when the latter was president of the NHL.

According to Red, media honourees were to receive the Elmer Ferguson Award and, with it, full membership in the Hall of Fame. But in the mid-nineties, the people who run the Hall took measure after measure to segregate the media and to dilute the nature of their status. They say that full membership in the Hall was never really accorded to the media, only associate status.

As part of that movement, the media were no longer given a blazer with the "honoured member" crest on the breast pocket. The crest now says, "Media honouree." They are no longer given a Hall of Fame tie, which had also been a part of the process. Most importantly, instead of being inducted with the players during the evening ceremony, as had been the case, they were shunted to a luncheon.

At one Hall of Fame board meeting, which is supposed

to be private but details invariably leak out, Boston Bruins general manager Harry Sinden complained vehemently about the fact that I had been wearing an honoured-member blazer at an induction ceremony. Well, I didn't make the blazer myself. Or the crest. The Hall gave it to me.

Still, I have never worn it since, and it was apparently because of Sinden's complaints that the rules regarding the status of media honorees were changed.

● ● ●

In 1993, as was the format in those days, all the inductees were honoured at a luncheon on the day of the ceremonies.

The late John D'Amico was being honoured that year and if there were ever a linesman truly worthy of induction, it was D'Amico. He was always aware of the moment, not just the game itself, and he was the one who made the famous call against Don Cherry's 1978 Boston Bruins for having too many men on the ice. He had spotted the infraction right away, but with time winding down in the seventh game of a Stanley Cup semi-final, he wanted any call that he made to be fully deserved. Finally, when the Bruins showed no sign of getting the offending player off the ice, he looked at Cherry, shrugged and made the call. Cherry nodded in acceptance.

D'Amico's strength was legendary among the players. When John D'Amico stepped into a fight to restrain you, you could consider yourself fully restrained. But he was also a gentle man, and during the brief speech that each of us gave at the luncheon, he was overcome by the honour and broke into tears.

Also being inducted that year was Billy Smith, the winner of four Stanley Cups as goaltender for the New York

Islanders. For good reason, he was known as "Battling Billy." On one occasion, when Montreal's Rejean Houle strayed too close to the crease, Billy gave him a butt end that opened a cut which required twenty-two stitches to close.

Goalmouth scrums were just as much a part of hockey then as they are today, the only difference being that in his era, Smith was rarely a non-participant. Billy began his speech by saying that he too, like the other inductees, was honoured to have been selected.

"And it's heart-warming to see John D'Amico in tears," he continued. "I even felt a tear or two myself when John was talking. But I have to say that John has often had me in tears. Of course, I was in a headlock at the time."

•   •   •

For years, some of the more sought-after assignments for hockey writers were the Toronto Maple Leafs' west-coast trips.

Frequent-flyer miles had nothing to do with it. Well, not a lot anyway. Well, not as much as the sports editor thought. (Now there are three words you rarely see in sequence.) All that aside, the trips were coveted because the Leafs invariably did something stupid—okay, more stupid than usual—and provided all kinds of material to write about.

One time, for instance, three players were wandering around downtown Los Angeles outside the Marriott LAX hotel (where all the hockey teams stayed). It's not the most genteel area in the world, and the three were robbed at gunpoint. They turned over all their valuables and it was widely opined that whatever the robber might have been after, it certainly wasn't Stanley Cup rings.

On another occasion there was something of a flap because goaltender Grant Fuhr wasn't on the Vancouver-bound plane out of Winnipeg. The obvious assumption was that something serious must have befallen him. After all, if it hadn't, it would be the first time that anyone had missed a plane *out* of Winnipeg.

Then there was the time during a team meal in the hotel where goalie Allan Bester and enforcer John Kordic got into a scrap. There weren't any media present but it was reliably reported from those on the scene that the scrap was a good one and that the two had a vigorous exchange and were rolling around on the floor. It could only have been better, the viewers said, had there been someone likeable to cheer for.

One night in Los Angeles, the players trooped out to a Mexican restaurant that was fortuitously located across the street from Harry O's, a sport bar partly owned by the former New York Islanders star Billy Harris.

Ken Yaremchuk, influenced by—among other things perhaps—the restaurant's Spanish theme, did his Manolete routine on the street outside. He was the toreador; the cars rushing past on the street were the bulls. He was relieved of his cape—and briefly of his freedom—by the unamused local police.

The long litany of Leafs foibles on the west coast even goes back to the seventies when Dave "Tiger" Williams and George Ferguson had a disagreement concerning the nature of Ferguson's pre-game preparation.

The two were roommates, and Williams hid Ferguson's shoes so that he couldn't go out on the town. Ferguson took exception to Tiger's *in loco parentis* attitude and a fight ensued.

Williams was a veteran of many hockey fights in which he had emerged unscathed, but in this one, he broke his hand when he took a swing at Ferguson, missed and punched the wall.

• • •

An incident that could have had much more serious ramifications took place during a road trip to San Francisco in 1993.

The team stayed at an elegant San Francisco hotel, but the neighbourhood had become run down in the decades since the hotel had been built. In short, the area in which it sat was downright dangerous. Darryl Shannon and Todd Gill went out for dinner, and when they staggered out of their taxi on the return trip, one of them accidentally jostled a passer-by.

Words were exchanged and a wrestling match ensued, but the hotel's doorman stepped in and the affair seemed to have reached its conclusion.

But both players had been carrying overcoats and jackets, and once they got into the hotel, they realized that Shannon's jacket, which had his ID and credit cards in the pocket, was missing. They went back outside, spoke to one of the many street people in the area and were directed to a nearby diner. Gill went inside to ask about the jacket. Outside the diner, one of the street people came up and told Shannon that the man who had taken his jacket was just around the corner in an alley.

Shannon immediately ran off down the alley. When Gill exited the diner, he couldn't find Shannon, but was told by yet another street person where he had gone. Gill found

Shannon in the alley on his hands and knees, bleeding and barely conscious. He was taken to hospital by ambulance and the police were summoned.

As it happened, the credit cards were lost, but Shannon's ID was retrieved. Wendel Clark bought it off another one of the street people. Shannon suffered a broken nose and a facial cut that needed a few stitches.

The next day, before the team bus left for the arena, a veteran San Francisco police officer came aboard and warned the Leafs not to treat downtown San Francisco as if it were Disneyland. Nice advice, but a bit late for Shannon.

Soon after, the San Jose Sharks moved their home games out of San Francisco's Cow Palace and into their new arena in San Jose, so the Leafs never stayed in downtown San Francisco again.

• • •

Todd Gill was one of the really good guys on that Leafs team. He wasn't the greatest player in the world, but he never floated, and if he made a mistake he never tried to put the blame on someone else.

When Wayne Gretzky was organizing his Scandinavian goodwill tour during the 1994 lockout, he and I sat on a Los Angeles-bound plane with Mike Barnett (his agent at the time) and tried to put together a list of players who would be good to take along on the trip.

As we named players, Barnett phoned them using Gretzky's credit card. Considering the cost of air-to-ground telephone calls in those days, Gretzky's telephone bill that month must have been higher than the gross national product of some emerging nations.

We had the rosters of all the teams in the league and were scanning them for likely names and I said, "What about Mario?"

Lemieux was out of hockey that year and neither Gretzky nor Barnett had considered him. But they thought his inclusion would be a great idea and Gretzky immediately gave him a call.

Lemieux declined, but later, when someone in the Quebec media decried the lack of French-Canadians on Gretzky's team, I let it be known that one of the very first guys to be called was Mario. That took some of the heat off.

The only other guy I suggested that they hadn't thought of was Todd Gill, and he was delighted to get the call. He not only made the trip, he quickly became one of the most popular guys on the team.

• • •

That trip took place in December 1994, and we came back just before Christmas. As is often the case, card games broke out on the flight and one foursome—Al MacInnis, Rob Blake, Marty McSorley and Todd Gill—were playing euchre.

I went wandering by at one point and MacInnis asked me if I wanted to take over for him. They were playing for $100 a game he said, but he was up $200 and I'd take over with a $200 credit. We had flown from from Switzerland to Reykjavik, Iceland, then to Goose Bay, Labrador. We were now on the third leg, heading for our destination of Detroit. I was Gill's partner and we won the next game. And the next. Now we were up $400 and the time left in the flight was getting shorter. Blake wanted to play one final hand, double or nothing. We did. They lost.

"Just one more hand," said Blake. "Definitely the last. Double or nothing."

We did. Now we were up $1600.

"This is it," said Blake. "The last hand. For sure. Absolutely."

Now we were up $3200.

"Okay," said Blake. "This is really the last one. We'll be landing soon."

"Robbie," I said, trying hard not to envision a Christmas with $3200 to spend on presents, "we can't keep on doing this. Eventually, you guys will win one."

"Okay," he said, "let's just play for $1000."

There was agreement all around. We played and we lost. Now we were up $2200.

By this time, the pilot had already announced that we had started our approach into Detroit and that we should act accordingly.

"Okay," said Blake. "We've only got time for one more hand. This will have to be the last one, we don't have any choice. Double or nothing,"

We were playing as quickly as we could and the score got to be 9–8 for them. But Gill and I got a hand that was an easy two-pointer. We were going to win $4400. Nothing to it. Because we were already on our approach, we were trying to hurry. We quickly rattled off all five tricks and said, "Okay. That's it. We win."

"Todd led out of turn," said Tony Granato.

Tony Granato? you might say. What's he got to do with it? He's not in the game. And had you been there, you would have been echoing my opinion. But Granato was standing in the aisle watching and had decided to offer his interpretation of the rules of euchre.

"It couldn't possibly make any difference," I said. "We had all the trumps between us. What difference does it make whose lead it was?"

McSorley and Blake were adamant. The lead had been out of turn, they said, and therefore we could claim only one point. With the score 9–9, we played one more hand as the plane was touching down and they won.

So much for a very merry Christmas. Thanks, Tony.

THIRTEEN

Falling out with Brian Burke...
again and again

At one point, I used to get along with Brian Burke. That was until he became general manager of the Vancouver Canucks.

Then it became apparent that he considered himself to be above criticism. He made a mess of the Pavel Bure deal and he mistreated Mike Keenan, a good friend of mine. When he became GM, Burke had inherited Keenan and had consistently said that he would give Keenan a reasonable amount of time after the Bure matter had been resolved before he would make any decision regarding Keenan's future as coach.

Thanks to Burke's hardline stance, Bure sat out more than three months of the season, so it was only fair that Keenan be given a chance to work with the full team.

But Burke broke his word and fired Keenan less than a week after moving Bure.

In my column for the *Toronto Sun*, I had no choice but to be critical of Burke for the trade—which was a poor one for the Canucks, to say the least—and I was also critical of him for his treatment of Keenan.

A columnist doesn't write the headlines for his columns, but the copy editor who did it in this case was right on the nose. The main head was "Burke blows it again." The over line was "Canucks GM botches Keenan firing, Bure trade."

I said that the week had been "a disaster for Burke—a poor return for his most marketable asset followed by an unnecessary coaching change handled in a totally inept manner."

After that we never got along.

• • •

The next blow-up came when I said on *Hockey Night in Canada* that I had been told that Brendan Morrison, one of Burke's players on the Canucks, was available.

Two NHL general managers had told me that, one in the east and one in the west.

Burke blew a gasket, saying that I had lied, that Morrison was not available.

First of all, I didn't lie. I had been told that Morrison was available. Perhaps the people who told me that were wrong, but that's another matter altogether.

It must be said that Burke is not very popular among his peers. It is quite possible that these GMs floated this story out there just to upset Burke. I know that neither GM was a great fan of his, and one told me that when the annual GM meetings were held, he and a few friends would sit at the back and laugh at Burke's non-stop pronouncements on the state of the game.

But whether the Morrison story was or was not true, a simple, mature option was available. It's one that most GMs use. They call the person who floated the story and tell him he was wrong. Then, at the next available opportunity, a correction is made.

It's not an option Burke has been known to use.

• • •

The dispute that most people remember should never have happened.

Burke had been on a flight with some *Hockey Night in Canada* people and had been showing them the contract he hoped to get from the Canucks. The information was passed along to me and I said on "Hot Stove" that he was looking for something in the $2-million range.

In those days, we usually taped the show in the afternoon because John Davidson had to do colour on the New York Rangers games at night. We did the show, then I went right to the Toronto airport. I was flying to England that night.

When Burke saw the "Hot Stove" segment, he flew into a rage. As soon as the game, which happened to be in Vancouver, was finished, he stormed downstairs and demanded that he be given airtime to call me a liar.

A more resolute producer would have told him to take a hike. Certainly John Shannon would have. But this was Joel Darling. He not only allowed Burke to deliver his rant, he even delayed a commercial break so that Burke wouldn't be inconvenienced.

Burke said that he would produce the contract, and if it had a 2 in it, he would resign.

He was safe in doing that. He was the general manager of a Canadian team, living in Canada and bragging about becoming a Canadian citizen. The show was on a Canadian network being broadcast to Canadians. I was talking about Canadian money—the same stuff Burke wanted to give Pavel Bure. He was asking for American money.

There was not a 2 in the contract. But according to Stan McCammon, the chief operating officer of the Canucks who later fired Burke, it came close to Can$2 million when it got converted.

• • •

Burke has a standard modus operandi when he encounters a media person who points out his failings. He tries to get him fired.

He even does it if he perceives some sort of slight to his organization. A radio announcer he got fired in Vancouver made a remark about Todd Bertuzzi's wife, not about Burke.

Burke even tried to get Don Taylor fired in Vancouver. There are few friendlier, more easygoing guys than Taylor. Burke tried to get him fired anyway.

Vancouver *Province* columnist Tony Gallagher is certainly not easygoing. He hammered Burke for his failings, with the usual response. Gallagher says that Burke approached the sports editor of the *Province* to get Gallagher fired. When that failed, he approached the managing editor. Still encountering no success, Burke moved up to the publisher of the paper, Dennis Skulsky.

Burke invited Skulsky out for lunch and immediately demanded that Gallagher be fired. When Skulsky refused, Burke threatened to pull all Vancouver Canucks advertising from the *Province*.

Skulsky told Gallagher that he said, "Brian, we can go to war over this if you want, but I don't see how it does either of us any good." Gallagher stayed on the job.

Time and again, I'd go to the CBC studios on a Saturday and be told by the executive producer that Burke had been calling during the week and complaining about my comments.

In the weeks immediately preceding his appointment as the Maple Leafs' GM, *Hockey Night in Canada* tried to get him to do an interview. He refused, saying that he would never appear on any show that employed me.

The ultimatum was clear. *Hockey Night* could either get rid of me or do without any Burke interviews.

Eventually, Burke did his interviews. He couldn't resist. No matter how great the terrorist threats might be in this country, there is still no more dangerous place to be than between Brian Burke and a working TV camera.

But he did his interviews on the tenth floor and I was dispatched to the fifth.

● ● ●

After two weeks of Burke's first full season as GM of the Leafs, I was fired. Prior to the season, we had all been given a schedule that had me doing the show all through the regular season, and to this day no one at the CBC has complained about my on-camera work.

Final thoughts

Hockey writers have a curious form of camaraderie. Close friendships exist between people who live in far-flung cities and see each other at irregular intervals.

For three or four days—or perhaps even for weeks, depending on the event—they would be together every night. Then the event would end, people would go home and not see each other again for six months. At large events like the draft, the Stanley Cup finals, the all-star game and so on—most of the serious hockey writers are in attendance. In the evening, large groups would invariably meet for dinner, then adjourn to a favourite watering hole.

In Edmonton during the dynasty years of the mid-eighties, the pub of choice was the Sherlock Holmes. In Los Angeles, it was the Melody Tavern. In Minneapolis, it was Juke Box Saturday Night. For years, we'd all go to Grumpy's on Bishop Street when we were in Montreal. At that time, a large number of hockey writers harboured the ill-conceived notion that they could sing, and in a move not at all likely to encourage their regular clientele, places like Grumpy's used to let us have a singalong. Grumpy's even went so far as to let us use their tape deck. I would take along a stack of sixties tapes on the road trip, then we'd quaff a few pints and sing along with the music. Even though we managed to organize the choir by ourselves, we had to submit to a higher power during the 1987 Canada Cup. Mike Keenan was coaching Team Canada and because he knew that hockey writers tend to be out late, he scheduled practices for mid-afternoon. That greatly endeared him to us, so when he showed up at Grumpy's and appointed himself choirmaster, there was little we could do. Terry Jones of the *Edmonton Sun* was designated as bass. Lance Hornby of the *Toronto Sun* had to do the whee-oos, a staple of songs by the Beach Boys. Others were assigned their various duties and because I knew all the words, I was told I had to be the lead singer. The problem is, I can't carry a tune.

Keenan, who is also a great aficionado of sixties music, would stand in the middle of the group like a maestro, pointing to the person who was due to make a contribution and generally demanding a level of excellence that was not really part of our repertoire.

If you screwed up, he'd grab your arm or chest and pinch. Every morning, I'd wake up covered with bruises.

• • •

Our greatest moments came when we performed "Paradise by the Dashboard Light," the classic by Meat Loaf. Even after we got away from taking tapes on the road, if we were in a bar with a jukebox, we'd play that song and sing along.

At the Nagano Olympics, we even chipped in to buy a ghetto blaster and the Bat Out of Hell tape so we could sing along. A lot of acting goes into a good production of that song, and over the years, we had some women who did a magnificent job playing the female role. Wendy Long from the Vancouver *Province* was one of the best. Christie Blatchford of the *Globe and Mail* is no slouch either. For a while, a Boston reporter named Wendy Butler was showing great promise, but in what we all considered to be a poor evaluation of her priorities, she moved to England. A couple of girls who used to hang around the Sherlock Holmes in Edmonton, Tammy Clarke and Melissa Guenette, were superb. Even Keenan didn't have much to complain about when we did that song. In fact, Bill Tuele, the long-time PR director for the Edmonton Oilers, listened to us do it one night and decreed it to be better than the Meat Loaf version.

That wasn't true. But we were pretty good. Then again, it was long ago and it was far away and it was so much better than it is today.